All inquiries should be addressed to:
American Culinary Federation
10 San Bartola Drive
St. Augustine, FL 32086
(800) 624-9458 • (904) 824-4468
acf@acfchefs.net
www.acfchefs.org

70 Years of Pioneering and Professionalism: A Celebration of Culinary Excellence by the American Culinary Federation
by Barbara Bell Matuszewski for American Culinary Federation

ISBN 0-9673403-0-6

Printed in the United States of America

TABLE OF CONTENTS

Welcome to
70 YEARS OF PIONEERING AND PROFESSIONALISM!

This book is a tribute to the founders of the American Culinary Federation. And, perhaps even more significantly, this book is a celebration of cooking—in particular, the delicious, innovative cuisine with which distinguished American chefs consistently delight customers and clients.

As members of ACF, we are culinary professionals—that is, chefs and culinary educators, students, and apprentices. Our careers are devoted to creating flavorful, enjoyable, nutritious foods and helping others master this skill. And, along the way, we derive one of our greatest joys from passing on our knowledge and expertise.

This book is also a milestone for ACF. Never in its 70-year history has the largest organization of professional chefs in the United States taken such a dramatic step outside the foodservice industry, by sharing our knowledge of foods and cooking techniques—especially our recipes—with all people who savor wonderful meals and/or love to cook.

Researching, compiling, and writing *70 Years of Pioneering and Professionalism* has been a labor of love that evolved following a 1998 forum for ACF national officers, committee chairs, and national staff. During those profoundly productive two days, we focused on our desire to ready ourselves to meet the professional demands of the coming new century; yet we also re-endorsed the principles and high standards of our founders and re-dedicated ourselves to continuing to meet both members' and consumers' needs today.

Thanks to productive input from hundreds of ACF members—plus intelligent, positive brainstorming by all those assembled—we were able to establish an achievable action plan that is now in effect and working. This book is an integral part of that program and of our commitment not only to serve culinary professionals but also to please our customers and clients.

Yes, *70 Years of Pioneering and Professionalism* is indeed a celebration of ACF's past. But, it is also a profile of its present, and certainly a harbinger of a future brimming with culinary delights conceived and created by America's most talented, most knowledgeable chefs.

Welcome to our kitchens and our recipes!

Noel Cullen, Ed.D., CMC, AAC
President
American Culinary Federation

A Note to Readers

The national staff of the American Culinary Federation is profoundly pleased to see the "idea" of an ACF cookbook become a reality. Elected officers have spent hours selecting their favorite recipes for inclusion in this volume, for which we thank them sincerely. Whether you are a professional culinarian or an amateur cook, you are certain to be inspired by the artistry of these renowned chefs.

In the past 70 years, ACF has emerged from an afternoon meeting of nine professional chefs who wanted to establish "an elite body" that would foster cooperation between employers and ACF, and would create and supervise the training of chefs by professionals. The organization long ago achieved its founders' goals. Today its influence stretches across the United States and even into the Caribbean, encompassing more than 300 chapters and 25,000 members—all of whom are chefs, culinary educators, and students and apprentices who are participating in ACF-accredited training programs.

We hope that you find the pages of this book interesting and informative for many years to come.

Terri L. Pittaro
Director of Operations
American Culinary Federation

Dedication

This book is dedicated to professional chefs since the first member of this highly skilled, singularly talented profession said to himself or herself, "I want to create food that people will enjoy eating, that will not only furnish sustenance but will also delight their senses and create cherished memories of delicious experiences."

This book is also dedicated to the 25,000 professional chefs, culinary educators, and culinary students who are members of the American Culinary Federation. For nearly two decades, they have generously shared their knowledge and experiences with me. I would not be entitled to call myself a professional food writer today had not so many proud, gifted, distinguished culinarians allowed me to visit their kitchens and classrooms, to observe their demonstrations, to listen to their critiques, to sit in on their meetings, to attend their conferences and conventions, and to ask them hundreds (perhaps thousands) of questions about the techniques of food preparation. Every contact with an ACF member has taught me something, including the fact that professional chefs rank as the world's most caring, loyal, and dedicated friends.

Barbara Bell Matuszewski

Acknowledgements

Text written and recipes edited by Barbara Bell Matuszewski.

Editorial support and advice provided by Wendy Philcox, editor, *The National Culinary Review*.

Liaison with ACF officers provided by Beverly Stuart, deputy director of operations, American Culinary Federation.

Book design and production by Publishing Partners, Inc., St. Augustine, FL.

Photographs of food prepared from elected officers' recipes by Ron Manville, Scituate, RI.

Food prepared from elected officers' recipes and photographic styling for photographs of all 20 of these dishes by Noel Cullen, Ed.D., CMC, AAC, and Laird Livingston, CEC, CCE.

Historical research for photography and procurement of historical photographs provided by Barbara Kuck of Johnson & Wales Culinary Archives and Museum, Providence, RI, and by Martin Olliff, archivist at Auburn University, Auburn, AL, and trustee of ACF archives.

The author/editor also acknowledges the contributions of ACF's ten elected officers whose recipes this book features. In addition, she is grateful to Terri Pittaro, ACF director of operations, and members of the staff of ACF national headquarters for their support and cooperation; the word "no" is not included in the vocabulary of this exceptional team.

Foreword

To my colleagues in the American Culinary Federation:

As ACF members, you are truly fortunate that your elected officers are uniquely dedicated to serving your many culinary interests. As demonstrated by their exceptional recipes that appear in *70 Years of Pioneering and Professionalism,* the directors of your federation also rank among the world's most accomplished, most innovative chefs. Long after their ACF terms of office have expired, these pages will remain a practical, useful, inspirational resource, not only for you but also for consumers throughout the United States. Your officers are to be commended on their selfless efforts to share culinary knowledge with all those who wish to learn.

With professional pride and pleasure, I offer you my congratulations on the 70th anniversary of the founding of your federation and on the extraordinary collaborative effort of researching, compiling, writing, and editing this commemorative text.

My best wishes to everyone who reads this book: professional culinarians who work as chefs and culinary educators; future professional culinarians who, as students and apprentices, aspire to careers in this honorable and rewarding profession; and amateur culinarians—home cooks, weekend cooks, and hobbyist-cooks—throughout the United States who, while striving to create flavorful, nutritious, enjoyable meals for their families and friends, delight in the joys of kitchen creativity.

Good reading and good cooking!

Bill Gallagher
President
World Association of Cooks Societies
Parklands, South Africa

LEARNING FROM *Yesterday*
TO ACHIEVE *Today*

The American Culinary Federation was conceived by a small group of courageous, forward-thinking chefs who were not unlike the bands of 18th- and 19th-century pioneers who forged westward across the North American continent to pave the way for the Atlantic-to-Pacific development of the United States. The ACF story, however, began much later, in 1929 in the city of New York, when nine renowned chefs gave birth to the unique federation whose members now, 70 years later, number some 25,000 culinarians who belong to 311 chapters in every state of the nation.

The reasons ACF's founders committed themselves to establishing and fostering the organization are written, both explicitly and between the lines, in the minutes of the federation's meetings during its first five years. Brittle and yellow with age, these hand-typed pages, probably hunted and pecked on an ancient manual typewriter, were composed by men who were far more skilled in culinary arts than in stenography and English grammar. Yet, they recorded in detail discussions at all official gatherings—except their first meeting—as well as legwork and paperwork that led to the historic launching of ACF.

Although the founders bequeathed us little information about conversations at their initial conclave in New York on May 20, 1929, they did provide a list of attendees and the names of the prestigious chefs' organizations that they represented:

- Louis Jousse, John Massironi, and Charles Schillig of the Chefs de Cuisine Association.
- Rene Anjard, Joseph Donon, and Louis Paquet of the Societé Culinaire Philanthropique.
- Charles Bournez, Charles Lepeltier, and Charles Scotto of the Vatel Club.

Interestingly, most members of the Chefs de Cuisine Association were Italian-born, while members of Societé Culinaire Philanthropique and the Vatel Club were predominantly French.

Even so, three and a half years later on behalf of the founders, Bournez wrote an editorial in which he expressed the wish that the federation could have immediately drawn members from many ethnic backgrounds and from other major American cities. As it was, Bournez later reported, "It took six years of continuous effort to convince the (New York) chefs of the utility of a federation, which could efficiently represent the three most important culinary groups." Thus, in its infancy, ACF functioned simply as a medium that morally united the three founding organizations.

Minutes of ACF's first ten meetings, in 1929 and 1930, report that the

FUTURISTS

Founding members of ACF represented three prestigious chefs' organizations, all based in New York: Chefs de Cuisine Association, Societé Culinaire Philanthropique, and the Vatel Club. Three of the nine founders are pictured below.

CHARLES SCOTTO

JOSEPH DONON

LOUIS PAQUET

MEETING OF SOCIETÉ CULINAIRE PHILANTHROPIQUE—ONE OF THREE ORGANIZATIONS THAT FOUNDED ACF—HOTEL ASTOR, NEW YORK, 1939.

During his long and brilliant culinary career, AUGUSTE ESCOFFIER *(1846-1935) was esteemed as "emperor of the world's kitchens." He created countless recipes, refined and defined French cuisine, operated dining rooms for Europe's finest hotels, and wrote several culinary textbooks including* Le Guide culinaire *(1903), a treatise for chefs;* Le Livre des menus *(1912); and* Ma cuisine *(1934).*

founders worked tirelessly to achieve three goals:

1. To create and maintain "an elite body of skilled 'cuisiniers.'"
2. To foster cooperation "between employers and ACF."
3. To establish and supervise "the training of cooks" under the guidance of a recognized professional organization, rather than by unqualified individuals.

From the outset, Scotto presided at meetings. During ACF's first two years, the chefs who would become the federation's original officers wrote a constitution and bylaws, incorporated, invited culinary organizations throughout the country to join them, and, on January 14, 1930, conducted their first election. Scotto was named president; Paquet and Massironi, vice presidents; Jousse, general secretary; and Schillig, general treasurer.

Taking great pains to uphold the traditions of the organizations that ACF members represented, officers unanimously and graciously awarded Societé Culinaire Philanthropique "the right to its annual exposition" and each of the three founding organizations "the right to hold its annual ball."

By January 29, 1931, Otto Gentsch of the Chefs de Cuisine Association held Jousse's seat on the board, Bournez had replaced Jousse as secretary, and Massironi had succeeded Schillig as treasurer. In addition, Boston's Epicurean Club had joined ACF, and officers were considering the "establishment of branches."

Massironi's financial report at that afternoon meeting explained how ACF had spent $339.75 of its initial $600 funding (which had been provided as a loan of $200 from each of the three founding societies): $300 for a charter and $39.75 for printing and miscellaneous expenses.

Thirteen days later, when the board met on February 11, correcting a misconception led the agenda. The Chefs de Cuisine Association of California had written to inquire

whether ACF was connected with the American Federation of Labor. Secretary Bournez hastened to reply negatively, explaining that ACF is "a national association of professional chefs and cooks, not a labor union."

That day, too, the secretary read a plan for an "apprenticeship system in American kitchens" that had been devised by the Epicurean Club. With few revisions, the outline was approved "in principle."

Eight days later, on February 19, the board met again to discuss details of apprenticeship—length of training, wage and bonus scales, the need for "a basic standard of cooking," how to launch the plan, and testing methods. Members agreed to one year in the pastry shop, followed by two years in the kitchen, with the provision that employers might shorten an apprenticeship or increase a salary based on individual ability. Afterward, a letter was sent to "all hotel and restaurant men explaining the stand ACF is taking."

The subjects of apprenticeship and education continued to dominate the next several board meetings. On March 3, Secretary Bournez recommended that *A Guide to Modern Cookery* by Auguste Escoffier, translated from French into English and published in 1909 by William Heinemann of London, be adopted as textbook for the ACF apprentice course. Surely this proposal pleased founders Scotto and Donon, both of whom had studied and cooked under Escoffier when, from 1898 to 1921, the *maître* was in charge of the kitchens at London's Carlton Hotel. In fact, only a year earlier in 1930, Escoffier (then past 80) had sailed to New York for the opening of the Hotel Pierre—a personal tribute to Scotto, who had been appointed the Pierre's first chef.

In 1931, the ACF board also appointed a committee of pastry chefs, to develop a plan for training "pastry men." By the end of March, three pastry chefs had met with the board, at which time President Scotto pointed out the need for better methods of training "cuisiners and patissiers. The education of our men," he said, "must be done by their natural leaders, by all those who have shown special ability and skill . . ." That pastry chefs teach the skills

A MAGNIFICENT BUFFET BY HERMANN RUSCH, AAC, CHEF DE CUISINE OF THE SWISS PAVILION RESTAURANTS AT THE 1939 WORLD'S FAIR, WON THE GRAND PRIX DE CUISINE AT THAT YEAR'S NATIONAL HOTEL EXPOSITION.

DINNER RULES OF LES AMIS D'ESCOFFIER SOCIETY OF NEW YORK, CIRCA 1939

The napkin must be tucked under the collar. Persons under the influence of liquor will not be permitted to sit at the table.

The wines, carefully selected to accompany and enhance the delicacy of each course, must be drunk during the course for which they are intended. To enforce this ruling, the glasses—even if full—will be removed at the end of each course. Smoking is absolutely forbidden up to the time dessert is served. A person who smokes while eating does not deserve the title of "Gourmet."

A WARNING

Since the "Les Amis d'Escoffier" Society is dedicated to the art of good living only, it is forbidden, under threat of expulsion, to speak of personal affairs, of one's own work or specialty, and more particularly to attempt to use the Society as a means of making business contacts. It is unnecessary to elucidate further upon this delicate subject which everyone understands. Furthermore, at these dinner-meetings reference will never be made on the subjects of: politics, religious beliefs, personal opinions of either members or guests irrespective of their profession or social status.

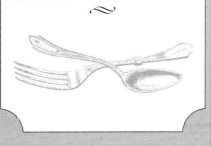

essential to their profession, he added, is only right and proper. Copies of a proposed instruction manual were distributed, and the guest chefs were asked to review the section covering pastry training.

On April 8, the board adopted the introductory chapters of its training manual, "composed with the help of Escoffier's *A Guide to Modern Cookery*." And, the group went on record as desiring a closer relationship with the Federation Culinaire Mondiale de Paris, the Geneva, the Helvetia, the Greeters, and similar organizations, with Secretary Bournez suggesting that a reception and ball be held jointly with ACF by these groups.

At meetings on February 26 and March 18, 1932, the board voted to begin producing a magazine. ACF would edit and control content. The secretary would coordinate material from sponsoring organizations. News, recipes, official reports, and articles "dealing with matters pertaining to the welfare of the profession" would be featured in each issue. English would be the official language. And, the magazine would be sold to nonmembers of ACF for 15 cents a copy or $1.50 per annual subscription.

That spring, when ACF was three years old, it had increased its membership to about 2,500 "men of good standing and professionally the best . . . in America," wrote Bournez. But all was not well. The federation was faced with investigating rumors that employers might, because of the Great Depression that was to permeate the 1929-1939 decade, lengthen back-of-house hours and, possibly, eliminate days off. Also, the board met with members of the International Cooks Association of Frankfurt, Germany, to effect "better representation of the New York culinary elements." ACF President Scotto assured ICA representatives that, regardless of nationality, in ACF, all members "have equal rights."

In the fall of 1932, a new concern surfaced. Salaries and maximum working hours for chefs and skilled cooks (in other words, executive chefs) earning $35 per week and more had been "deliberately omitted by the Government Code." ACF officers also found that the Hotel Industry Code contained unacceptable clauses relating to hiring and firing, hourly wages, apprentices, and working hours. A delegation representing ACF, therefore, travelled to Washington, D.C., and delivered to the U.S. Bureau of Labor a memorandum outlining "the way a man should be trained to be qualified either as a cook or a chef." ACF Secretary Bournez later reported, "This is the first time that such

KITCHEN STAFF OF SWISS PAVILION RESTAURANTS AT NEW YORK WORLD'S FAIR IN 1940; HERMANN RUSCH, AAC, CHEF DE CUISINE, STANDS IN CENTER OF BACK ROW.

28TH ANNUAL GALA DINNER DANCE OF THE CHEFS DE CUISINE ASSOCIATION AT THE PLAZA HOTEL, NEW YORK, OCTOBER 2, 1954. MENU AT RIGHT.

data have been furnished to the Bureau of Labor and will certainly help to place the chefs and skilled cooks in the professional category." Little did Bournez know that 45 years would elapse before the U.S. Department of Labor's *Dictionary of Occupational Titles* would officially elevate chefs from domestics to the ranks of professionals!

On October 1, 1932, ACF published the first issue of its magazine, then called *The Culinary Review.* In it, G. A. Halletz explained that the thrust of editorial content would be "food, its preparation, the true values of foods, and the secrets of culinary art as created by the greatest food authorities: the chefs de cuisine of America and the world." Halletz also outlined *The Review's* purposes: encouragement of interest, welfare of culinary crews, "promotion of due respect to culinary art and its masters," better-trained cooks and kitchen personnel, closer contact between guests and chefs, better employment conditions, and getting "the right man to the right job." He praised ACF officers who "with energy and self-sacrifice created this educational magazine" and "built a monument for themselves which will be appreciated and respected by our successors for centuries to come."

For the inaugural issue, Phileas Gilbert, author and editor of *Revue Culinaire de Paris,* wrote a congratulatory article in which he expressed the hope that the two publications would work together for the benefit of the culinary profession. In addition, essays from members of ACF's founding organizations explained membership criteria and emphasized the cooperation and support each was enjoying through ACF membership.

That issue's lead feature was headed "La Page du Maitre." The message, which had been dispatched from Monte Carlo and appeared on page nine, was from the 86-year-old master, Auguste Escoffier, who wrote to proclaim his "belief in the ACF cause" and to send greetings, wishes for success, and three menus to his "dear colleagues and friends in the United States."

Secretary Bournez reported that *The Review's* inaugural issue received many compliments, plus one complaint about some articles, including Escoffier's, printed in French. Replied Bournez, "We do hope that in the future more... will be published in English . . . (meantime) we must be patient and tactful."

LE MENU

LE CONSOMME DE VOLAILLE AUX QUENELLES, REMINI PAILLETTES FINES CROUSTILLANTES
(double chicken broth with forcemeat puffs, crisp butter sticks)

LE ROI DES CRUSTACES, MONSEIGNEUR LE RIZ PILAFF
(lobster meat sautéed, flamed with aged Armagnac brandy, fresh tomatoes and a tang to tease your palate—fluffy rice)

LE TOURNEDOS AUX CEPES PROVENÇALE LE COEUR DE CELERI BRAISE AU JUS
(heart of prime beef tenderloin sautéed with fine herbes, flavored with Alpine mushrooms, braised celery)

LES AIGUILLETTES DE CANETON VOISIN ACCOMPAGNEES D'UNE BONNE SALADE PASCALINE
(supreme of duckling with gooseliver and truffles, both imbedded in port wine jelly and masterfully decorated—also a delightful mixture of romaine, endives, hearts of palm with special vinegar and olive oil)

LE BISCUIT GLACE PLAZA SUR SOCLE ILLUMINE LES FRAISES NOUVELLES ARROSSEES DE LIQEURS RARES LA CORBEILLE FLEURIE DES MIGNARDISES
(a dessert of frozen Marsala sabayon mixed with whipped cream, served with fresh strawberries, flavored with rare liquors and to the tunes specially arranged for this timely presentation)

ACF MEETINGS

Although 1999 marks ACF's 70th anniversary, the July 1999 annual national convention is only the 49th. The first two were in New York in 1938 and 1950. Since, 1953, a convention has been held every year—in cities from Honolulu to Washington, from Chicago to San Antonio.

~

FIRST CULINARY CONGRESS IN THE U.S.A.
Sponsored by
The American Culinary Federation Inc., and "Culinary Review"
at the Waldorf-Astoria — November 6th to 9th, 1939.

REPORTAGE IN THE CULINARY REVIEW OF THE FIRST CULINARY CONGRESS IN THE UNITED STATES, WALDORF-ASTORIA, NOVEMBER 6-9, 1939.

DINNER FOR SECOND CULINARY CONGRESS, SEPTEMBER 26, 1950, IN THE HAWAIIAN ROOM, HOTEL LEXINGTON, NEW YORK.

FORMER PRESIDENT HARRY S. TRUMAN WAS IN BOSTON FOR A SPEAKING ENGAGEMENT WHEN ACF WAS CONDUCTING ITS 1956 NATIONAL CONVENTION AT THE SOMERSET HOTEL THERE. CHEF LOUIS TURCO, ACF CONVENTION CHAIR, AND THE HOTEL STAFF WELCOMED THE UNEXPECTED GUEST WHEN HE DROPPED IN AT AN ACF DINNER.

By 1933, ACF was operating a placement bureau whose services were free to both employers and applicants. The federation was also the only organization in the United States whose members were chefs de cuisine exclusively. And, by then, ACF proudly counted among its members both native- and foreign-born chefs, all of whom the organization regarded as "the elite of the culinary profession."

Additional accomplishments during the 1930s include ICA and other chefs' organizations joining ACF, emergence of large culinary shows, launching of an apprenticeship program, and introduction of the ACF seal of approval.

In 1937, Scotto, first president of ACF, died. For the next 16 years, Donon, as general secretary, managed the federation—without a president.

Throughout World War II, ACF meetings were curtailed, and the federation regularly sent packages of food and supplies to Europe and the South Pacific. When the war ended in 1945, ACF business resumed. By 1950, the organization had four chapters (in Pittsburgh, St. Louis, Boston, and Philadelphia); two years later, it had 15 chapters.

ACF arranged its first two national conventions in New York in 1938 and 1950. Prior to the September 25 through 27 gathering in 1950—at various locations, including the Food Trades Vocational High School in Manhattan and the Culinarians' Home Foundation in New Paltz, NY—Edouard Panchard, editor, expressed the purposes of the convention in that month's issue of *The Culinary Review.* The ACF convention, he wrote, "through understanding, confidence, and enthusiasm, can reinforce the solid foundations upon which (the federation) has been built and thus promote the best interests of the culinary profession and, in particular, the interests of its members in that time-honored profession."

National leaders of ACF, Panchard continued, understand "modern progressive methods" in the foodservice industry and are "free from individual idealism or bias." In addition, he wrote, ACF can foster good will toward "the culinary profession and bring about a closer spirit of cooperation and unity of action that must

IN 1954, OTTO GENTSCH, AN ACF DIRECTOR IN 1931, AND HERMANN RUSCH, AAC, A LONGTIME ACF MEMBER, CELEBRATED GENTSCH'S BIRTHDAY WITH CAKE AND A HANDSHAKE.

60th ANNUAL AMERICAN CULINARY FEDERATION NATIONAL CONVENTION

PRESIDENTIAL
GOLD PLATE DINNER
JULY 26, 1989

LOBSTER BOUQUETIERE
HERBED DUCK STRUDEL
CASSIS SORBET
VEAL CHOP STUFFED with
SUN DRIED TOMATO DUXELLE
SPINACH and RADICCHIO
CHAMPAGNE SHALLOT VINAIGRETTE
VIENNESE PASTRIES
COFFEES of the WORLD

CAESARS PALACE

THE 1955 ACF CHARITY BALL, BENEFITTING THE CULINARIANS' HOME FOUNDATION IN NEW PALZ, NY, WAS HELD AT THE HOTEL STATLER, NEW YORK.

ACF HAS PUBLISHED
a magazine since 1932.

1946

1956

1958

1977

1984

1991

1999

eventually result in that single-mindedness of purpose which makes for successful teamwork." Certainly Panchard's message is as accurate and appropriate in 1999 as it was in 1950.

At the third national convention in Pittsburgh in 1953, Paul Laesecke, AAC, was elected the first president of the federation since the death of Scotto. The following year, in Washington, D.C., 250 delegates representing 16 chapters named Pierre Berard, AAC, president. That year, ACF had 18 chapters; six years later, in 1960, 20 chapters were flourishing.

Since 1953, ACF national conventions have been conducted annually in cities throughout the United States. At the 1962 convention in Dallas, Willy Rossel, AAC, chair of ACF's history committee, was elected ACF president. That year, too, a new on-the-job training manual was produced with the help of a grant from the American Hotel/Motel Association.

One of the most distinguished achievements of ACF during this period was its establishment in 1955 of the American Academy of Chefs. Peter Berrini, AAC, organized ACF's honor society and was named its first chair, which position he held until 1959 when he was elected ACF national president.

Throughout the 1960s, ACF contined to expand its rosters of members and of chapters. During that decade, too, the former all-male persona of ACF, as well as of the culinary profession itself, gradually began to change as increasing numbers of women were apprenticed, educated, and earned well-deserved professional stature in foodservice kitchens.

In 1969, L. Edwin Brown, who retired in 1995 as executive vice president of ACF, began working with ACF chefs in Pittsburgh. Brown's 30-year association with ACF would eventually rise to the national level and continues, in one function or another, even today.

In the 1970s, ACF made major strides in serveral operational areas. For one, the American Institute of Chefs merged with the federation in 1970. For another, in 1973, under the banner of the American Culinary Federation Educational Institute, Brown taught the first certification class and placed the first 24 apprentice-graduates. Meantime, at that year's national convention, the new program spelling out criteria for certification—in particular, required

ACF HEADQUARTERS BUILT BY STUDENTS

Although founded in 1929, ACF had no permanent home until 53 years later. Before that, ACF records were shuttled from city to city after every election. In 1991, the late Baron H. Galand, CEC, AAC, then chairman of the board, described the system as a "shoebox operation."

Most ACF records were housed with sitting presidents. Handwritten (sometimes typed) names and addresses of members and chapters, financial statements, minutes, reports, etc., were maintained by ACF officers. After each election, outgoing officers shipped dozens of "shoeboxes" and other containers filled with paper records to their successors.

In 1980, the board voted to establish a national office. St. Augustine was chosen as the site mostly because that city's proposal included the donation of one acre of land.

In 1981, ACF broke ground for the first commercial building erected in Florida by construction students. In November 1982, L. Edwin Brown, executive director, and three other employees moved into the not-quite-finished structure. A few weeks later, Brown hired Beverly Stuart, now deputy director of operations, as assistant bookkeeper. ACF's staff has since grown to 27.

Now a modern, efficient organization that operates with the latest electronic equipment, ACF has come a long way since its years as a "shoebox operation."

~

JOHN BANDERA, CEC, AAC; RICHARD BOSNJAK, CEC, AAC; HARRY HOFFSTADT, CEC, AAC; C. ORBY ANDERSON, CEC, AAC; FERDINAND E. METZ, CMC, AAC; AND L. EDWIN BROWN CUT RIBBON AT DEDICATION OF HEADQUARTERS, MAY 1982.

SEVERAL PROMINENT EARLY ACF LEADERS JOIN IN A 1971 CELEBRATION OF THEIR INDUCTION AS MEMBERS OF THE HONORABLE ORDER OF THE GOLDEN TOQUE, AN HONOR SOCIETY AFFILIATED THROUGH MULTIPLE PERSONAL RELATIONSHIPS TO ACF.

points and classes, including nutrition and sanitation—had been adopted. From 1975 to 1988, Brown served as chair of ACFEI, and from 1977 to 1979, he directed the national apprentice program and its six regional offices.

In addition, during this decade, a growing coterie of female culinarians was earning professional recognition. Among them was Lillian Haines, CEC, AAC, who, in March 1976, became the first woman elected to AAC membership.

Four years later, at the 1980 Culinary Olympics in Frankfurt, Germany, for the first time, another woman—Lyde Buchtenkirch-Biscardi, CMC, AAC—represented the United States on an ACF culinary team. She won gold medals for her garde manger platters and dough sculpture. To this day, she is the only female who is a certified master chef. And, incidentally, on her CMC examination in 1990, she earned the highest score in her group of candidates.

The 1980s saw the certification of ACFEI's first five master chefs and the establishment of a national headquarters for ACF. Brown resigned from his community-college teaching position in Pittsburgh early in 1980 and moved to St. Augustine, to oversee the building and establishment of ACF national headquarters, which would open in 1982. At that time, the national staff included Brown and three employees. The only computer on the premises—by today's standards, certainly a primitive model, perhaps best described as a typewriter with memory—was used to maintain membership records. Once the names of all paid-up members had been fed into the system, the ACF board learned that the federation had about 5,000 members, not 10,000 as earlier hand-written records had suggested.

Today, in its 17-year-old national headquarters in St. Augustine, ACF continues to grow—not only in numbers of members and chapters, but also in services, strength, recognition, and prestige. Members are ever appreciative of the accomplishments of the pioneering founders and the remarkable chefs who have led the federation for the past 70 years.

PAST *Presidents* SERVE AS *Role Models*

When a president of ACF steps down, he assumes the position of chairman of the board for the next term of office. Certainly, after that assignment, no past president has ever retired from taking an active role in the administration of ACF. Instead, all have continued to lead, advise, assume responsibilities as committee chairs, originate and develop food-preparation techniques, advance in their careers, and serve as paragons of the culinary professionalism. Indeed, the roster of ACF past presidents lists 19 of the world's most distinguished, most accomplished chefs.

ACF Past Presidents are Culinary Innovators

Typical of ACF past presidents, Keith Keogh, CEC, AAC (1991-1993), does not rest on his culinary laurels. He is president and CEO of California Culinary Academy. He teaches, serves on ACF committees, presents seminars, arranges scholarships, and moderates ACF's annual Baron H. Galand Culinary Knowledge Bowls that test—*Jeopardy*-style—and reward the knowledge of culinary students all over the United States. Among Keogh's many culinary innovations is top-of-stove suspension-smoking for larger cuts of meat, poultry, and fish. Keogh's recipe and instructions appear on page 16.

Two other remarkable chefs who have served as presidents of ACF—John L. Bandera, CEC, AAC (1964-1967), and Richard Bosnjak, CEC, AAC (1975-1979)—have also furnished recipes that they originated some years ago. These instructions also appear on page 16.

IN THE 1980S, THE LATE PAUL LAESECKE, AAC, SECOND PRESIDENT OF ACF, POSED WITH A BRONZE BUST OF HIM THAT IS DISPLAYED PERMANENTLY AT NATIONAL HEADQUARTERS.

PAST PRESIDENTS

In the past 70 years, the leadership of 20 exemplary chefs (including Noel Cullen, Ed.D., CMC, AAC, current president) has helped ACF earn designation as **the** *authority on food in America.*

1929-1937
*Charles Scotto**

1953-1954
*Paul Laesecke, AAC**

1954-1956
*Pierre Berard, AAC**

1956-1959
*Eugene Ertel**

1959-1960
*Peter Berrini, AAC**

1960-1962
*C. Orby Anderson, CEC, AAC**

1962-1964
Willy Rossel, AAC

1964-1967
John L. Bandera, CEC, AAC

1967-1973
*Jack Sullivan, AAC**

1973-1975
Amato Ferrero, AAC

1975-1979
Richard Bosnjak, CEC, AAC

1979-1983
Ferdinand E. Metz, CMC, AAC

1983-1987
*Baron H. Galand, CEC, AAC**

1987-1991
Jack F. Braun, CEC, AAC

1991-1993
Keith Keogh, CEC, AAC

1993-1994
Michael Ty, CEC, AAC

1994-1995
John Folse, CEC, AAC

1995-1996
L. Timothy Ryan, CMC, AAC

1996-1997
Reimund D.Pitz, CEC,CCE, AAC

*deceased

**Recipe by John L. Bandera, CEC, AAC
1964–1967 ACF President**

BASIC MEXICAN SALSA
6 TO 8 PORTIONS

INGREDIENTS
- 8 ripe tomatoes, peeled, seeded, and diced
- ¼ cup chopped fresh cilantro
- 7 jalapeños, diced
- 1 medium red onion, diced
- ¼ cup garlic, finely chopped
- 1 small red bell pepper, diced
- 1 cup olive oil
- 3 cups tomato juice
- 4 tablespoons ground cumin
- 1½ teaspoons salt
- 1 teaspoon ground black pepper
- 1 teaspoon crushed oregano
  juice of 3 limes

METHOD
In a bowl, mix ingredients until well-blended. Refrigerate 2 hours. Serve with grilled meats.

**Recipe by Richard Bosnjak, CEC, AAC
1975–1979 ACF President**

MARYLAND-STYLE CRAB CAKES
4 PORTIONS

INGREDIENTS
- 1 teaspoon Old Bay seafood seasoning
- 1 teaspoon Coleman's dry mustard
- ¼ teaspoon salt
- 1 tablespoon mayonnaise
- 1 tablespoon Worcestershire sauce
- 1 tablespoon chopped fresh parsley
- 1 tablespoon baking powder
- 1 egg, beaten
- 3 slices bread, crusts removed and moistened with a little milk
- 1 pound lump blue-claw crab meat
  clarified butter as needed

METHOD
Thoroughly combine all ingredients except crab meat and butter. Mash to the consistency of a paste. Gently fold in crab meat. Shape into 8 patties.

Heat enough butter to cover a skillet well. Fry patties until golden brown on each side, turning once. Serve immediately.

**Recipe by Keith Keogh, CEC, AAC
1991-1993 ACF President**

WOOD-FIRED SALMON
8 TO 10 PORTIONS

INGREDIENTS
- 7 pound whole fresh salmon, including 6 to 8 ounces fat-free scraps (cheeks, head, and trimmings)
- 1 egg white
- 5 fluid ounces (⅝ cup) heavy cream
- 1 tablespoon chopped fresh tarragon
- 4 ounces bay scallops, poached, cooled, and diced
- 4 ounces slipper lobster tails, poached, shelled, cooled, and diced
  salt and pepper as needed
  cooking oil as needed
- 3 cups apple- or alder-wood chips

METHOD
Fillet, debone, and skin fish. Scrape all meat from bones and save. Refrigerate fillets.

In chilled bowl of food processor, pulse scraps 30 seconds until meat begins to ball. Add egg white; process about 10 seconds until incorporated. Through feed tube, slowly add cream. Stop motor; scrape bowl with rubber spatula. Pulse 3 more times. Pass forcemeat through sieve into chilled bowl. Fold in tarragon, scallops, lobster, salt, and pepper. Refrigerate until cold.

Place forcemeat in pastry bag. Pipe onto inside of one fillet (the side removed from the skeleton); spread with spatula. Place second fillet on forcemeat, inside down, in opposite direction of bottom fillet—with head at tail end, tail at head end. Press firmly together so no pockets form in forcemeat and fillets are sealed to each other.

Soak 2 pieces of 2½" butcher's netting in oil; place on sleeve. Season fish with salt and pepper; run through netting twice to form 2 layers. Outside layer will support fish and hold dowel.

Place chips in 6" hotel or other deep pan; set over heat on flat top or buner of stove so chips begin to smolder. Using 2 strips of metal or wood as rack, place fish several inches above chips, hanging on rack supported by dowel. Loosely cover with another pan. Smoke 30 minutes. Then set entire container in 375°F oven for 25 minutes. Remove; let rest 10 minutes. Remove netting; cut into two 2½-to 3-ounce slices per portion.

70 Years of
PIONEERING AND PROFESSIONALISM

ELECTED NATIONAL OFFICERS 1997-1999
Who THEY ARE, WHAT THEY DO *Best*

*N*ational officers of ACF are elected by federation members. Every active member of the organization is entitled to a full vote, every student member a half-vote.

The full slate of 10 officers includes president; chairman of the board, who is also the immediate past president; four vice presidents, each representing an ACF region (central, northeast, southeast, and western); secretary; treasurer; chair of the American Academy of Chefs; and secretary-treasurer of AAC.

No officer of ACF is paid for his or her services. Each, however, devotes untold hours to the functions of his or her office and, at the same time, pursues an active, demanding career as a professional chef or culinary educator. In addition, several officers operate their own successful consulting and/or catering businesses.

ACF officers accumulate thousands of frequent-flyer miles each year, as they travel from their home-bases to participate in regional conferences, board and committee meetings, forums, workshops, seminars, an annual national convention, and other ACF events that require their time and attention. In addition, they are always accessible to members—to attend chapter meetings, to solve problems, to furnish information, to answer questions, and to advise and mentor.

Members are the life's blood of ACF. Elected national officers are the arteries through which that blood is circulated to every nook and cranny of the ACF network.

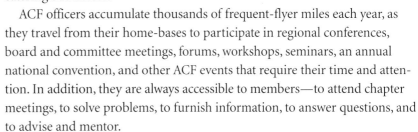

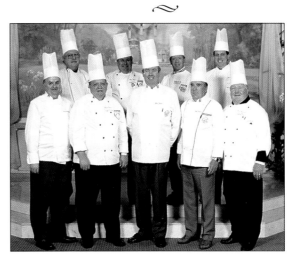

NINE OF ACF'S 1997-1999 ELECTED NATIONAL OFFICERS (L. TO R.): MICHEL D. BOUIT, CEC, AAC; JOHN KINSELLA, CMC, CCE, AAC; GEORGE J. PASTOR, ED.D., CEC, CCE, AAC; DERT P. CUTINO, CEC, AAC; NOEL CULLEN, ED.D., CMC, AAC; REIMUND D. PITZ, CEC, CCE, AAC; BOB CHESTER, CEC, CCE, AAC; EDWARD G. LEONARD, CMC, AAC; AND KLAUS D. FRIEDENREICH, CMC, AAC. ABSENT FROM PHOTOGRAPH: FRITZ SONNENSCHMIDT, CMC, AAC

PRESIDENT

Noel Cullen, Ed.D., CMC, AAC

Associate Professor

School of Hospitality Administration

Boston University

Boston, MA

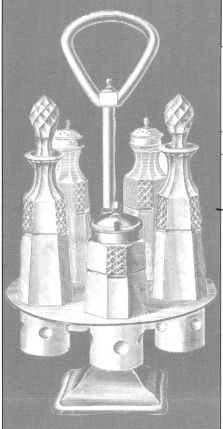

MARINATED PAN-SEARED LAMB LOIN WITH POTATO CROQUETTES

ELECTED NATIONAL OFFICERS 1997–1999

Noel Cullen
Ed.D., CMC, AAC

WHO THEY ARE, WHAT THEY DO BEST

A native of Ireland who began his chef's apprenticeship there at age 13, Dr. Cullen now teaches culinary arts, food and beverage management, and human resources management. He has earned both foodservice and education degrees, including the licentiate of the City and Guilds of London Institute, a master of science degree, and a doctor of education degree. For more than 30 years, he has been employed in the fields of foodservice, hospitality, hospitality-administration, and education as a culinarian, chef patron, executive chef, manager, and associate professor.

Cullen is recipient of an impressive list of professional citations and awards. He is a certified master chef. He has earned more than 45 international prizes for his culinary skills, including seven gold medals at the Culinary Olympics. At the 1988 event in Frankfurt, Germany, he served as captain of the U.S. Confrérie de la Chaîne des Rotisseurs team that won 27 gold medals and two grand prizes. For three years, he coached Team USA Northeast, which earned 22 gold medals in a series of international competitions, culminating at the 1992 Culinary Olympics, also in Frankfurt.

He has been elected to memberships in the American Academy of Chefs, the Honorable Order of the Golden Toque, Les Amis des Escoffier Society, and Confrérie de la Chaîne des Rotisseurs. He is also a fellow in the Epicurean World Master Chefs Society, and past chairman of the American Culinary Federation Educational Institute. He is a member of ACF Rhode Island Chapter.

ACF cited Cullen as national educator of the year (1995). Le Salon Culinarie de Londres accorded him its professional services award (1996), and the Council on Hotel, Restaurant & Institutional Education its Chef Herman Breihapt trophy for excellence in hospitality education (1997). The Craft Guild of Chefs has named him a master craftsman, and Johnson & Wales University has awarded him three distinguished visiting chef chairs. He has also been a principal speaker at the National Restaurant Association show (1996).

Cullen is author of the following books: *The Principles and Practices of Culinary Arts*; *Life Beyond the Line: A Front-of-House Guide for Culinarians*; *Team Power: Managing Human Resources in the Hospitality Industry*; and *The World of Culinary Supervision, Training, and Management*. Currently, he is writing three additional books, including one titled *Elegant Irish Cooking*.

GRILLED GUINNESS-MARINATED
SIRLOIN STEAK

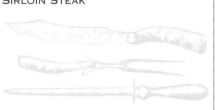

MARINATED PAN-SEARED LAMB LOIN
4 PORTIONS

INGREDIENTS
   vegetable oil as needed
 2 sprigs fresh thyme, diced
 ½ teaspoon chopped fresh basil
 ½ teaspoon chopped fresh rosemary
 1 bay leaf
 1 boneless loin of lamb, trimmed
    of all fat and skin
 1 small red bell pepper
 1 small green bell pepper
 1 small yellow bell pepper
   salt as needed
   freshly ground pepper as needed
 1 clove garlic, crushed
 1 teaspoon chopped fresh rosemary
 2 shallots, finely diced
 ½ cup dry red wine
 ½ cup demi-glace
 1 tablespoon butter
 4 large portobello mushrooms,
    cleaned
 1 tablespoon melted butter

METHOD
For marinade, mix 1 cup oil, thyme, basil, rosemary, and bay leaf. Add lamb; cover and refrigerate for 2 hours.

Cut peppers lengthwise into quarters; remove seeds. Brush a little oil over skin sides of peppers; place on sheet pan. Broil until skins begin to burn. Immediately transfer to a plastic bag and seal. Refrigerate 10 minutes.

Remove peppers from bag. Scrape off burned skin and discard. Julienne peppers.

Remove lamb from marinade; season to taste with salt and pepper. Season with garlic and rosemary. In a skillet, sear in 1 tablespoon of marinade oil over high heat. Then bake at 375°F for 3 minutes. Remove from pan; keep warm.

Discard oil from skillet. Add shallots. Deglaze with wine and reduce by ⅓. Stir in demi-glace, simmer briefly, and strain.

In a saucepan, sauté peppers in butter for 10 seconds.

Brush mushrooms with melted butter; grill 1 minute on each side (or bake in 400°F oven).

On each plate, set 1 mushroom in center. Arrange ¼ of peppers on top. Carve lamb loin on bias; arrange noisettes on peppers. Pour a ribbon of sauce around lamb. Serve with potato croquettes (see recipe page 21).

PORK TENDERLOIN WITH SAGE AND ROASTED GARLIC
2 PORTIONS

INGREDIENTS
2 pork tenderloins, about 6 ounces each, trimmed of excess fat
1 tablespoon fresh sage leaves
3 cloves garlic, sliced
½ cup + 2 tablespoons olive oil
about 1 cup dry white wine
3 whole heads of garlic
1 tablespoon vegetable oil
1 shallot, finely diced
1 cup chicken stock
1 teaspoon chopped fresh sage
2 tablespoons unsalted butter
salt as needed
freshly ground white pepper as needed

METHOD
Place pork in a glass baking dish. Add sage, sliced garlic, ½ cup olive oil, and enough wine (about ½ cup) to cover meat. Cover; marinate in refrigerator overnight.

With a sharp knife, cut about ½" off top of each garlic head. Arrange in shallow baking pan. Drizzle remaining 2 tablespoons olive oil evenly over garlic. Bake uncovered at 350°F for 45 to 60 minutes until soft, brushing often with oil.

Remove meat from marinade; pat dry with paper towels. In an ovenproof skillet, heat 1 tablespoon vegetable oil. Add pork; brown on all sides. Bake at 350°F for 10 minutes or until meat is cooked to desired degree of doneness.

Remove meat from pan. Discard grease in skillet. Add shallot; cook until golden brown. Add remaining ½ cup wine; reduce by ¾. Add stock; reduce by ½. Add chopped sage and butter; cook until smooth, stirring constantly. Season with salt and pepper.

Squeeze garlic from cloves; with a fork, mash to a paste.

For each portion, arrange thinly sliced pork in a circle on a warm serving plate. Place half the garlic in center of circle. Pour sauce over meat and serve at once.

ROASTED GARLIC-CHIVE ROYALE WITH WILD MUSHROOM CONFIT
4 PORTIONS

INGREDIENTS
1 whole head of garlic
olive oil as needed
1 tablespoon chopped fresh chives
2 cups heavy cream
salt as needed
¼ teaspoon ground nutmeg
freshly ground pepper as needed
pinch cayenne pepper
1 tablespoon butter
4 medium eggs
1 pound wild mushrooms: chanterelles, morels, shiitake, and oyster mushrooms
2 shallots, sliced
8 fresh basil leaves, shredded
1 teaspoon chopped fresh parsley
4 medium scallions, sliced lengthwise

METHOD
Cut about ½" off top of garlic. Place in shallow baking pan; drizzle 1 tablespoon olive oil evenly over top. Bake uncovered at 350°F for 45 to 60 minutes until soft, brushing often with oil. (When cooked, garlic should be soft, mellow, nutty, and buttery.) Cool. Separate cloves. Squeeze garlic from skins and chop. Place in a medium saucepan with chives and cream. Simmer 3 minutes. Strain through a fine sieve; season with salt to taste, nutmeg, pepper to taste, and cayenne.

Lightly butter 4 ramekins or darioles.

In a bowl, whisk eggs; stir in garlic cream. Divide equally among 4 molds. Place molds in deep baking pan. Pour boiling water around molds until it reaches halfway up sides of molds.

Bake at 350°F for 20 minutes, or until firm to the touch. Remove from oven; cool slightly.

Wash and dry mushrooms; trim stems. Depending upon sizes, leave whole or cut into large pieces.

In a skillet over medium heat, sauté shallots in 2 tablespoons oil. Add mushrooms; saute 2 to 3 minutes. Season to taste with salt and pepper. Toss in basil and parsley.

For each portion, run the tip of a knife around the inside of a mold to free the royale. Unmold onto center of a warm plate. Spoon mushroom confit around royale. Garnish with sliced scallion.

~ 70 Years of ~
PIONEERING AND PROFESSIONALISM

CHICKEN BREASTS STUFFED WITH SMOKED SALMON COLCANON
2 PORTIONS

INGREDIENTS

1 large baking potato, scrubbed
1 quart salted water
½ cup washed, drained, chopped kale
1 scallion, finely diced
¼ cup + 1 teaspoon butter
2 ounces smoked salmon, finely chopped
2 boneless chicken breasts with skins on
    salt as needed
    freshly ground pepper as needed
1 teaspoon olive oil
2 tablespoons white malt vinegar
1 tablespoon finely diced shallots
2 tablespoons heavy cream
6 tablespoons unsalted butter, very cold and
    cut into pieces
2 tablespoons chopped chives

METHOD

Bake the potato at 475°F for 40 minutes until tender.

In a medium saucepan, bring salted water to boil. Add kale; cook for 20 minutes until soft. Quickly cool in ice water; drain and chop.

Cut potato in half; scoop out flesh, and mash. Discard skin or use for another purpose. Add scallion, ¼ cup butter, kale, and smoked salmon. Mix well. Refrigerate until thoroughly chilled.

Make an incision in the side of each chicken breast. Using a pastry bag, pipe potato mixture into pocket. Close with wooden toothpicks. Season with salt and freshly ground pepper.

In a heavy-bottomed skillet over high heat, sauté chicken in olive oil and remaining 1 teaspoon butter for about 15 minutes, turning to cook at least twice on each side. Keep warm.

In a small saucepan, cook vinegar and shallots over high heat, reducing liquid to 1 tablespoon. Add cream; thicken over gentle heat. Cool slightly; whisk in chilled butter pieces. Stir in chives.

For each serving, make a pool of sauce in center of a warmed plate. Discard toothpicks. Cut chicken breast in half; arrange halves on sauce.

GRILLED GUINNESS-MARINATED SIRLOIN STEAKS
4 PORTIONS

INGREDIENTS

1½ cups Guinness
1½ cups chicken stock
2 sprigs fresh thyme
1 teaspoon Worcestershire sauce
    freshly ground black pepper as needed
1 bay leaf
4 10-ounce sirloin steaks, well trimmed of
    fat and gristle
½ cup unsalted butter, cut in 4 equal pieces
2 large cooked potatoes, peeled and sliced
    lengthwise
1 clove garlic, crushed
1 teaspoon olive oil
    salt as needed
4 plum tomatoes, peeled, seeds removed,
    and cut in chunks
1 tablespoon chopped fresh chives

METHOD

For marinade/sauce, in a deep dish, thoroughly mix Guinness, stock, thyme, Worcestershire, ½ teaspoon pepper, and bay leaf. Completely immerse steaks in marinade, cover, and refrigerate for 8 hours.

Remove steaks from marinade. Pour marinade into a saucepan; bring to boil, skimming off surface foam. Reduce marinade by half. Remove from heat and strain. Whisk in butter, 1 piece at a time, until totally incorporated in sauce.

Grill steaks to desired degree of doneness.

Rub potatoes with garlic, oil, and salt and pepper to taste. Arrange in one layer on baking sheet; grill until golden brown on both sides, turning once. Arrange tomatoes on potatoes; sprinkle with chives.

Per portion, arrange ¼ of tomatoes/potatoes on one side of warmed plate. Lay 1 steak to the other side. Pour sauce around steak. Serve immediately.

POTATO CROQUETTES
10 PORTIONS

INGREDIENTS

2 pounds potatoes of uniform size
    water as needed
2 egg yolks
    salt as needed
    nutmeg as needed
    flour as needed
    egg wash as needed
    unseasoned fine dry bread crumbs as
      needed
    vegetable oil as needed

METHOD

Peel potatoes. Boil in water until tender. Drain. Return to pan and dry over very low heat.

In food processor, purée potatoes. Add egg yolks and incorporate. Season to taste with salt and nutmeg. Shape mixture into cylinders 1" thick x 3" long. Dip each in flour, egg wash, then crumbs. Deep-fry in oil until golden brown. Drain and serve with lamb loin (see recipe page 19)

SHRIMP WITH GARLIC AND PERNOD
4 PORTIONS

INGREDIENTS
2½ cups fish stock
8 tablespoons butter
1 tablespoon finely diced onion
6 ounces Arborio rice
1 teaspoon turmeric
¼ cup dry white wine
1 tablespoon grated Parmesan cheese
1 teaspoon chopped fresh parsley
1 tablespoon olive oil
1 shallot, finely diced
3 cloves garlic, crushed
32 large shrimp, peeled and deveined
1 tablespoon lemon juice
1 teaspoon finely chopped fresh tarragon
¼ teaspoon cracked peppercorns
⅛ teaspoon paprika
½ teaspoon Worcestershire sauce
1 teaspoon chopped fresh chives
¼ cup Pernod
⅔ cup heavy cream

METHOD
Bring fish stock to simmer.

In a heavy-bottomed saucepan, melt 4 tablespoons butter. Add onion; cook until soft but not colored. Add rice and turmeric; stir well to coat rice with butter but do not brown. Add wine; stir until absorbed. Add ¼ cup stock. Cook and stir until stock is absorbed. Repeat procedure, adding stock ¼ cup at a time, using a total of 2 cups stock, and cooking 18 to 20 minutes in all until rice is tender. Remove from heat; stir in 2 tablespoons butter, cheese, and parsley. Keep warm.

In a large, heavy-bottomed skillet over medium heat, melt remaining 2 tablespoons butter with oil. Add shallot and garlic; cook 30 seconds without coloring. Increase heat to high; add shrimp, lemon juice, tarragon, peppercorns, paprika, and Worcestershire. Stir and toss constantly for about 2 minutes. Stir in chives.

Move shrimp to one side of pan. Pour Pernod onto a dry section of pan; ignite for about 30 seconds. Add remaining ½ cup stock and cream; simmer 1 minute until thickened slightly.

Per portion, mold ¼ of rice in a small cup; invert onto center of a warm plate. Surround with 8 shrimp. Serve immediately.

STEWED RHUBARB WITH MUESLI TOPPING
4 PORTIONS

INGREDIENTS
whole hazelnuts as needed
2 teaspoons honey
½ cup water
3 cups young rhubarb, washed and sliced
¼ cup whole-wheat flour
¼ cup instant oatmeal
cinnamon as needed
¼ cup brown sugar, packed
¼ cup melted butter
whipped cream as needed

METHOD
Roast hazelnuts in 275°F oven for 12 to 15 minutes, until they just begin to darken. Remove from oven. While still hot, rub nuts in a dry towel to remove skins. Chop enough nuts to yield 1 tablespoon. Toast lightly in 425°F oven.

In a medium-sized saucepan over low heat, simmer honey, water, and rhubarb for 5 minutes.

In a bowl, mix flour, oatmeal, 1 teaspoon cinnamon, sugar, and hazelnuts. Stir in melted butter.

Arrange stewed rhubarb in a 6" x 6" x 2" casserole. Cover with flour mixture. Bake at 425°F for 10 minutes.

Flavor whipped cream with cinnamon. Serve a dollop on each portion of warm pudding.

BREAD AND BUTTER PUDDING WITH IRISH WHISKEY SAUCE
6 PORTIONS

INGREDIENTS
6 tablespoons sultanas or golden raisins
hot water as needed
¼ cup butter
1 pound white bread, sliced and crusts removed
2 cups milk
1 cup cream
1 vanilla pod
½ cup + 3 tablespoons sugar
3 eggs, beaten
2 egg yolks
¼ cup Irish whiskey

METHOD
Soak sultanas or golden raisins in hot water to cover for 10 minutes. Drain and dry.

Butter bread. Cut into triangles and arrange in a 6" x 6" x 2" casserole.

In a saucepan, bring 1 cup milk, cream, vanilla pod, and ½ cup sugar to just below a boil. Remove vanilla pod. Gradually add hot milk to beaten eggs, mixing thoroughly. Strain custard, add raisins, and pour over bread. Let soak 30 minutes.

Cover casserole with aluminum foil. Bake in a water bath at 350°F for about 55 minutes. Remove foil; bake 5 minutes to allow top to crisp.

In a saucepan, bring remaining 1 cup milk to boil; remove from heat.

In another saucepan, mix remaining 3 tablespoons sugar and egg yolks; add to milk and return to heat. Cook over low heat, stirring constantly until sauce thickens slightly. Stir in whiskey and serve on bread and butter pudding.

~ 70 Years of ~
PIONEERING AND PROFESSIONALISM

TRIFLE OF SALMON AND TUNA TARTARE

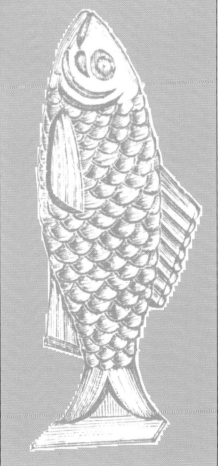

ELECTED NATIONAL OFFICERS 1997-1999

Reimund D. Pitz
CEC, CCE, AAC

WHO THEY ARE, WHAT THEY DO BEST

For 20 years, Pitz served as area chef, sous chef, chef de cuisine, and executive chef at Walt Disney World/MGM Studios theme park. When he resigned in 1996, he was responsible for 21 food outlets of various culinary styles—ranging from gourmet, executive, and celebrity dining to trendy meals and fast food—that produced in all as many as 32,000 meals per day and annual sales of $89 million. He supervised a staff of 842, including 58 management-level chefs. He was in charge of all food, labor, research and development, training, catering, nutritional content, and restaurant operations. In 1995, he reorganized and consolidated his staff and operations and saved the corporation some $4 million. When he was appointed executive chef, he was the youngest in WDW history.

In 1996, Pitz was named vice president of operations at the culinary arts training center of Southeastern Academy, with responsibility for the school's

BOYSENBERRY SOUP

entire food and beverage operation, including student feeding facilities and People's Place restaurant and bakery. Last year, however, he returned to his true love, the profession of executive chef, by accepting his current position at the Country Club of Orlando.

A member of ACF Central Florida Chapter, Pitz served as vice president of the ACF southeast region from 1993 to 1996. In 1996, he was elected ACF national president.

Trained as a chef in his native Germany, Pitz has earned many culinary awards, citations, and honors. In 1992, he was named southeast region and national ACF Chef of the Year. In 1991, he received both the southeast region and national ACF Chef Professionalism Award. He also won two consecutive Florida Governor's Cup Seafood Challenges, in 1990 and 1991. At the 1988 international Culinary Olympics in Frankfurt, Germany, he earned five gold medals, one perfect score, and the grand gold medal. He also helped lead 1992 Culinary Team USA to victory at the international Culinary Olympics, and, for 1996 Culinary Team USA, he served as advisor.

Pitz has earned 20 gold medals, seven silver, and two bronze. He is a recipient of an ACF President's Medallion. He is the youngest recipient of the Golden Toque Award, and he holds the Antonin Carême Medal. He has served as continental director of the Americas for the World Association of Cooks Societies since 1996, on the ACF culinary committee since 1991, and on the board of directors and advisory board of the ACF apprentice program since 1991.

COUNTRY-FRIED CHICKEN SALAD
6 PORTIONS

INGREDIENTS

8 cloves garlic, peeled and crushed with a knife
1 cup kosher salt
3¾ teaspoons freshly cracked black pepper
1 tablespoon minced fresh thyme
2 tablespoons finely chopped fresh sage
1 teaspoon ground nutmeg
½ cup + 1 teaspoon Dijon mustard
  freshly ground black pepper as needed
3 pinches cayenne pepper
2 boneless, skinless chicken breasts, each sliced on the bias into 4 pieces
2 boneless, skinless chicken thighs, each trimmed and sliced on the bias into 4 pieces
1 tablespoon red-wine vinegar
¾ cup extra-virgin olive oil
2 cups unseasoned fine dry bread crumbs
½ cup buttermilk
  salt as needed
6 thin slices pancetta or bacon
½ cup peanut oil
2 quarts salad greens (spinach, curly endive, baby lettuce, radicchio, et al.), cut in bite-sized pieces

METHOD

For seasoning salt, in food processor, process garlic, kosher salt, 2 teaspoons cracked black pepper, thyme, sage, and nutmeg. Pour into a jar, cover, and refrigerate until ready to use.

For marinade, in a stainless-steel bowl, whisk together ½ cup mustard, ½ teaspoon prepared seasoning salt, 1½ teaspoons ground black pepper, and 1 pinch cayenne. Flatten chicken with a mallet, coat with marinade, cover, and refrigerate until ready to cook

For vinaigrette, whisk together 1 teaspoon mustard, ½ teaspoon prepared seasoning salt, ¼ teaspoon cracked black pepper, 1 pinch cayenne, vinegar, and olive oil.

Season crumbs with salt and pepper. Remove chicken from marinade. Coat first with buttermilk, then with crumbs, pressing firmly into chicken. (Do not dip chicken in crumbs, as leftovers will be used as garnish ingredient.)

In a skillet, lightly brown pancetta; drain and crumble. Mix into leftover crumbs with 1 teaspoon prepared seasoning salt and remaining pinch of cayenne.

In a medium skillet, heat peanut oil until it almost smokes. Fry chicken in 2 batches until golden brown on both sides, approximately 20 minutes total. Drain on paper towels; keep warm.

Toss greens with vinaigrette. Per portion, arrange greens on a dinner plate. Position fried chicken pieces on top of greens. Sprinkle with pancetta-crumb mixture.

TRIFLE OF SALMON AND TUNA TARTARE
10 PORTIONS

INGREDIENTS

- 2 shallots, peeled and minced
  extra-virgin olive oil as needed
- 10 ounces fillet of yellowfin tuna, skinned
  and cut into small dice
- 3 tablespoons mustard-flavored oil
- 2 teaspoons lemon zest
- ¼ cup soy sauce
- 2 tablespoons chopped fresh cilantro
- 1 teaspoon coarse salt
- 2 pinches finely ground white pepper
- 10 ounces fillet of salmon, skinned and
  ground
- 2 teaspoons peeled, grated horseradish root
- 2 tablespoons chopped capers
- 2 tablespoons finely chopped fresh chives
  salt and pepper as needed
- 2½ tablespoons osetra or other dark caviar
- 2½ tablespoons salmon (red) caviar
- 1 cup crème fraîche
- 10 whole chives

METHOD

In a small saucepan, sauté shallots in 1 tablespoon olive oil until transparent.

In a medium bowl sitting on a bed of ice, combine half the sweated shallots, tuna, 1½ tablespoons mustard oil, 1 teaspoon lemon zest, soy sauce, 1 tablespoon oil, and cilantro. Season with coarse salt and white pepper; with a large spoon, mix well.

In another medium bowl sitting on a bed of ice, combine remaining half of sweated shallots, remaining 1½ tablespoons mustard oil, remaining 1 teaspoon lemon zest, and salmon. Mix until well-combined with 1 tablespoon olive oil, horseradish, capers, chopped chives, and salt and pepper to taste.

Line a sheet pan with waxed paper or parchment. With fingers, lightly oil insides of 10 2"-high x 2"-diameter metal rings or molds. Arrange rings on sheet pan.

Place 1½ tablespoons tuna mixture in each ring, smoothing top with back of a spoon. (Ideally, press down with bottom of a Worcestershire or Tabasco sauce bottle.) Then place 1½ tablespoons salmon mixture on tuna, pressing down and smoothing with back of a spoon. Spoon approximately ½ teaspoon osetra caviar on half the top of each ring, then approximately ½ teaspoon salmon caviar on other ½, smoothing with the back of a spoon.

Whip crème fraîche until thick, stiff peaks form. To each ring, add 2 tablespoons crème fraîche, smoothing with back of a flat knife or small metal spatula and making sure crème fraîche is level with top of mold. Refrigerate for at least 20 minutes, preferably 2 to 3 hours.

Per portion, place ring on a dinner plate. Gently remove mold by pulling ring upward, leaving trifle intact. Garnish each with one whole chive, placed at an angle over trifle.

ROASTED QUAIL WITH MUSHROOM RISOTTO
6 PORTIONS

INGREDIENTS

- olive oil as needed
- ½ large onion, peeled and finely diced
- 2 cloves garlic, peeled and minced
- 2 cups Arborio rice
- 1 quart chicken stock
- ¼ cup peeled, minced shallots
- ¾ pound mushrooms (cremini, shiitakes,
  and/or portobellos), cleaned, stemmed,
  and coarsely chopped
- ¼ cup unsalted butter
  kosher salt as needed
  freshly ground black pepper as needed
- 2 branches thyme
- 6 quails, boned and halved
- ½ cup chopped fresh herbs—equal parts
  tarragon, chives, and parsley

METHOD

For risotto, in a wide, hot saucepan, heat 2 tablespoons oil. Sauté onion and garlic until caramelized. Add rice, stirring in one direction only with a wooden spatula or spoon (to avoid breaking grains, which would make risotto gummy). Add ¼ cup stock, stirring constantly until liquid is almost absorbed and making sure rice does not stick to bottom of pan. Add ½ cup stock and repeat procedure until 2 cups stock (½ quart) have been added and absorbed.

In a skillet, heat 2 tablespoons oil. Add shallots and mushrooms. Saute until they begin to release liquid. Add to risotto. Add butter and, if risotto is too dry, more stock. Season to taste with salt and pepper.

To prepare sauce, simmer remaining 2 cups stock for about 30 minutes, until it is reduced to 1½ cups. Season to taste with salt and pepper. Infuse with thyme for 45 seconds; remove and discard thyme.

Rub quail with oil. Sprinkle with ¼ cup mixed herbs and salt and pepper to taste. In a hot skillet, heat 1½ tablespoon of oil. Sear quail for 2 minutes on each side. Bake in 350°F oven for 5 minutes.

To serve, divide risotto among 6 plates, spooning it into center. Arrange one portion of quail on each risotto bed. Spoon sauce over quail; sprinkle with remaining ¼ cup mixed herbs.

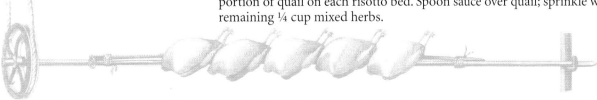

ROAST CHICKEN WITH MUSHROOM HASH
6 PORTIONS

INGREDIENTS

3 3½-pound chickens
   salt and pepper as needed
   water as needed
   cooking oil as needed
½ pound bacon, minced
2 large onions, peeled and minced
3½ pounds baking potatoes, peeled and diced into ½" cubes
2½ cups chicken stock
1 pound assorted wild and/or cultivated mushrooms, cleaned and sliced
1 cup heavy cream (optional)
1 or 2 tablespoons butter
2 tablespoons chopped fresh thyme
¼ cup chopped fresh parsley
1 pound spinach, thoroughly washed, drained, dried, and stems removed

METHOD

Remove wings and drumsticks from chickens. With a boning knife, remove breast and thigh in one piece from each side of each chicken. Season with salt and pepper. Make stock with wings, drumsticks, carcass, and water.

Heat a small amount of oil in a large skillet over high heat. Arrange chicken, skin sides down, in pan and cook, turning once, until skin is golden brown. Remove chicken to baking pan. Bake at 475°F approximately 30 minutes, turning once, until chicken is cooked through but still juicy.

Discard oil from skillet. Cook bacon until fat is ¾ rendered. Add onions, potatoes, and stock. Cook over low heat until soft. Add mushrooms and, if desired, heavy cream; cook until hash is barely moist. (If not using cream, add 1 tablespoon butter.) Salt and pepper to taste and stir in thyme and parsley.

In a medium skillet, melt 1 tablespoon butter; sauté spinach for a few minutes until al dente. Season with salt.

Per portion, place mushroom hash off-center on a dinner plate; top with chicken. Arrange spinach beside hash.

Note: If using dried mushrooms, soak in water to cover and add strained liquid with cream.

ROASTED BEET TERRINE
3 PORTIONS

INGREDIENTS

6 to 8 large fresh beets
   salt and pepper as needed
2 cups lobster or chicken stock
1 cup dry red wine
1¼ cups balsamic vinegar
1½ tablespoons granulated unflavored gelatin
10 leaves of Chinese cabbage
1 large leek, green tops removed and cleaned
   olive oil as needed
3 tablespoons prepared white horseradish, drained
2 cups crème fraîche
2 shallots, peeled and finely diced
   juice of ¼ large lemon
   coarse sea salt as needed
   freshly ground white pepper as needed
¼ pound smoked salmon, thinly sliced on the bias
3 tablespoons chopped Italian parsley
1 whole lemon

METHOD

Scrub beets; arrange in a shallow pan. Sprinkle with salt and pepper. Bake at 375°F until very tender, about 2½ hours. Cool. Peel and slice ¼" thick. 5 cups are required for recipe.

In a medium saucepan over medium-high heat, reduce stock, wine, and vinegar for approximately 30 minutes, until 1¾ cups remain. Season with salt and pepper. Add gelatin slowly in a fine stream, constantly whisking.

Blanch cabbage in boiling salted water for 3 to 4 minutes, until just tender; refresh in cold water. Drain, pat dry with paper towels, and reserve.

Split leek lengthwise, keeping root end together. Soak in warm water for 10 minutes. Drain and boil in salted water 8 to 10 minutes until tender. Drain; cool in cold water. Slightly trim root end, but not so that leek falls apart.

Lightly coat a 9" x 4" loaf pan with oil, or line with plastic wrap. Line bottom and sides of pan with cabbage leaves. Layer beats in pan until half-full. Set leek down the length of the center so that the root ends of each leek half touch each other as they did before splitting. Lightly season with salt and pepper. Pour in half the reduced stock. Layer remaining beets until loaf pan is level full. Lightly season with salt and pepper. Pour in remaining stock. (Set a spare cabbage leaf on top to fill, if there is a gap.) Cover with plastic wrap. Set on a shallow pan. Place a 1-pound weight (e.g., 1 quart of milk) on top of loaf. Refrigerate 6 to 8 hours or overnight.

For sauce, in a stainless steel bowl, whisk horseradish, crème fraîche, shallots, lemon juice, sea salt, and white pepper just to incorporate.

With a serrated or electric knife, cut terrine into ½" to ¾" slices. Place two slices in center of each plate. Spoon sauce at base of slices. Make a rosette from a salmon slice by rolling tightly from one end to the other; place next to sauce. Sprinkle parsley over and around beet terrine. Slice lemon into thin rounds or zest it. Garnish each plate with rounds or zest.

GRILLED VENISON CHOPS WITH WILD MUSHROOM PIE AND BLUEBERRY-GRAPPA SAUCE

4 PORTIONS

INGREDIENTS

- 3 tablespoons finely chopped fresh thyme
- 3 tablespoons finely chopped fresh tarragon
- 3 tablespoons finely chopped fresh Italian parsley
- 3 tablespoons finely chopped fresh chives
- 3 tablespoons unsalted butter
  extra-virgin olive oil as needed
- 1 shallot, peeled and minced
- 2 cloves garlic, peeled and minced
- 1 pound assorted wild mushrooms (morels, shiitakes, black trumpets, oysters, porcinis), cleaned and sliced
  kosher salt as needed
  freshly ground white pepper as needed
- 2 eggs + 1 egg yolk, beaten together
- 2 sheets phyllo dough, about 15" x 26", cut in half and, if frozen, thawed
- ¼ cup warm clarified butter
- ½ cup dried blueberries
- 1 cup fresh blueberries, washed and well-drained
- 1 sprig fresh thyme
- 1 cup blueberry wine or brandy
- 1 tablespoon sugar (more if desired)
- 3 tablespoons Muscato grappa
  vegetable or chicken stock if needed
- 4 center-cut venison rib chops about 1¾" thick, frenched
- ½ cup chopped fresh thyme

METHOD

Thoroughly mix chopped thyme, tarragon, parsley, and chives.

In medium-sized skillet, heat 1 tablespoon butter and ¼ cup oil. When mixture is just getting hot, add shallot and garlic. Cook and few seconds; add mushrooms. Season with salt and pepper. Sauté over low heat until mushrooms are tender; cook until juices have evaporated. Stir in ¾ of mixed herbs. Drain and cool. Mix with eggs and yolk.

Lay 1 half-sheet of phyllo on a hard surface, placing it so 15" side is horizontal. Cover with warm clarified butter. Sprinkle with 2 teaspoons reamaining mixed herbs. Spread mushrooms over ¾ of sheet, leaving 1" border on all sides. Tuck ends up over filling, as if wrapping a package; roll carefully. Place on baking pan, seam side down. Brush outside, including ends, with clarified butter. Repeat procedure with 3 remaining half-sheets of phyllo. Roll in plastic wrap and refrigerate until ready to use.

For sauce, in a small saucepan combine dried and fresh berries with thyme sprig and wine or brandy. (Add more wine or brandy in increments of 1 teaspoon if desired.) Sprinkle with sugar. Simmer until berries are soft and alcohol has evaporated. Transfer to blender. Add remaining 2 tablespoons butter. Process until smooth. Stir in grappa and, if desired, more sugar. Strain twice through a medium-fine sieve, pressing down with a spoon. If sauce is too thick, thin with stock. Cover; keep warm but do not boil.

Arrange phyllo rolls on a baking sheet. Bake at 350°F until golden brown on all sides, 12 to 15 minutes. Remove from oven; wait 2 minutes before slicing.

Allow chops to come to room temperature. Pat dry. Season lightly with salt and heavily with pepper and thyme, reserving a few pinches of thyme for garnish. Brush with oil; grill over very hot coals approximately 2 to 3 minutes per side for rare, longer for medium and well-done. (Chops may also be pan-seared in 1 tablespoon olive oil and 1 tablespoon butter.) Keep warm.

To serve each portion, spoon a pool of sauce on one side of a warm dinner plate. Arrange 3 slices phyllo, overlapping, on other side. Sprinkle entire plate with remaining thyme. Place a chop on sauce.

GRILLED MORELS WITH GARLIC, CHIVES, AND BALSAMIC VINEGAR
4 PORTIONS

INGREDIENTS

1½ pounds morels, cleaned and stems removed
2 tablespoons extra-virgin olive oil
2 cloves garlic, peeled and finely minced
salt and freshly ground black pepper as needed
¼ cup Italian parsley leaves, stems removed, and minced
¼ cup snipped fresh chives
¼ cup balsamic vinegar
4 chives or sprigs of parsley

METHOD

In a medium-sized bowl, combine morels, oil, and garlic. Season to taste with salt and black pepper, mixing well.

Spread morels evenly on pre-heated, oiled grill. Grill about 2 minutes, until well-seared. Turn mushrooms over with metal spatula or tongs. Cook another 3 minutes until tender. With a spatula, return mushrooms to bowl.

Add Italian parsley, chives, and vinegar; toss to combine well. Adjust seasoning.

Divide among 4 plates. Garnish with chives or parsley.

BOYSENBERRY SOUP WITH VANILLA ICE CREAM AND PEACHES
4 TO 5 PORTIONS

INGREDIENTS

3 cups ripe boysenberries (or substitute blackberries)
¾ cup water
9 tablespoons granulated sugar
½ teaspoon kirsch
6 ripe, juicy peaches, halved, pitted, and thinly sliced
1½ pints high-quality vanilla ice cream, preferably home-made
4-5 sprigs mint
accompaniment: 4 or 5 crisp cookies

METHOD

In non-corroding medium-sized saucepan, heat berries with water and 3 tablespoons sugar until sugar is dissolved. Remove from heat; strain through a fine sieve into a bowl, pressing with spoon. Add more sugar if desired. Stir in kirsch. Cover with plastic wrap. Refrigerate until very cold.

In a bowl, toss peaches with remaining 6 tablespoons sugar, using less or more to taste.

Divide soup among 4 or 5 bowls. Place a scoop of ice cream in center of each. Garnish with a mint sprig. Surround with sliced peaches. Serve immediately with a crisp cookie.

FALLING CHOCOLATE CAKES WITH RASPBERRY SAUCE AND VANILLA ICE CREAM
8 TO 10 PORTIONS

INGREDIENTS

1 quart + 1 cup fresh or frozen raspberries
1½ cups sugar
juice of ½ lemon
¾ pound semisweet chocolate
½ pound unsalted butter
½ cup all-purpose flour
6 large eggs
confectioners' sugar as needed
1½ pints vanilla ice cream
8-10 sprigs fresh mint

METHOD

For sauce, in a small saucepan, mix 1 quart raspberries, ½ cup sugar, and lemon juice. Boil until sugar dissolves. Cool. In a blender or food processor, purée half the sauce. Combine unpuréed and puréed sauce; cover and refrigerate.

In top of double-boiler over simmering water, melt chocolate and butter. Cool.

In bowl of electric mixer, beat remaining 1 cup sugar, flour, and eggs for 5 minutes, until very thick and fluffy. Fold in chocolate and butter. Cover and refrigerate until ready to use.

Pour chocolate mixture into 8 to 10 buttered individual ramekins, each about 3"x 2". Bake at 350°F for 15 minutes, until edges are firm yet center is loose.

For each portion, spoon a 4" round of sauce onto each plate. Remove cake from ramekin and place on sauce. Dust cake with confectioners' sugar. Place one scoop of ice cream next to cake. Garnish with a mint sprig and some of remaining 1 cup of raspberries.

~ 70 Years of ~
PIONEERING AND PROFESSIONALISM

CURRIED SWEET POTATO SOUP

SECRETARY

John Kinsella, CMC, CCE, AAC

Owner, Kincom Inc., Chef Preferred

Brands and Unique Solutions Inc.

Carmel, OH

and Chef/Instructor,

Cincinnati State Technical College

Cincinnati, OH

ELECTED NATIONAL OFFICERS 1997-1999

John Kinsella
CMC, CCE, AAC

WHO THEY ARE, WHAT THEY DO BEST

Since 1983, Kinsella has been responsible for practical and theoretic instruction in both the culinary arts and the hotel programs at Cincinnati State Technical College. The culinary curriculum, which is ACF-accredited, has earned two excellence awards from the state of Ohio.

Prior to joining the CSTC faculty, Kinsella was executive chef and food and beverage director of the Cincinnati Club from 1981 until the club was closed and sold in 1983. Earlier, he was part-owner of a catering business, executive chef of the Bankers Club, and executive chef of Cincinnati's Terrace Hilton. He also spent nine months in Louisiana learning Cajun and Creole cooking from John Folse, CEC, AAC.

From 1958 to 1974, as a member of England's Royal Air Force, he served as executive chef on royal flights and chef/instructor at the College of Catering in Hereford. During that period, he often cooked for the royal family and mem-

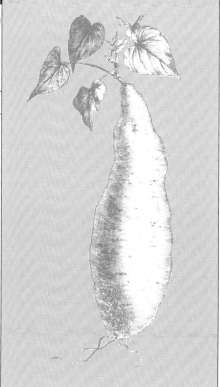

CHIPOLATA SAUSAGE

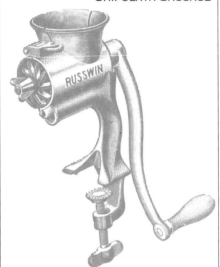

members of parliament, as well as for inflight and hospital feeding programs. He also participated in a number of other facets of foodservice. In 1964, he earned a teaching diploma at the RAF School of Education.

Kinsella completed his culinary apprenticeship at London's Grosvenor House Hotel, under Chef Rene le Bec, who had been apprenticed to Escoffier. He also earned his City and Guilds Certificates by studying at Westminster Technical College in London. In 1985, he earned ACF-certified master chef designation, in 1992 a magna cum laude AOS degree from CSTC, and in 1995 certification as a hospitality educator.

Kinsella has held the office of ACF national secretary twice, 1990–1992 and 1997–1999. He is former national chair of ACF's Chef of the Year committee and recipient of a President's Medallion. His chapter, ACF of Greater Cincinnati, elected him 1984–1989 secretary-treasurer and 1986 Chef of the Year. He also spearheaded the 1993 ACF Drive for the Hard Drive.

Winner of many medals, Kinsella competed on the RAF culinary team 1964 to 1970. Since 1983, he has coached and managed the CSTC junior team to 40 awards. He was manager of Culinary Team Midwest for the 1998 World Cup in Luxembourg. He is personal food consultant to the honorable Roxanne Qualls, mayor of Cincinnati; co-host of *Everybody's Cooking*, a weekly radio program; and author of three books: *Professional Charcutiere*, *The Spud Manual*, and *The Melting Pot*.

CURRIED SWEET POTATO SOUP
6 PORTIONS

INGREDIENTS
6 tablespoons butter
⅔ cup diced sweet onions
⅓ cup diced carrots
⅓ cup diced celery
1 tablespoon diced garlic
2 pounds sweet potatoes
1 teaspoon ground ginger
1 teaspoon dried red peppers
1 teaspoon curry powder
1 teaspoon cilantro
1 teaspoon sweet basil
1 teaspoon lemon thyme
3 pints chicken stock, heated
   salt and pepper as needed
8 ounces plain yogurt
8 ounces heavy or light cream or
   half-and-half (optional)

METHOD
In butter in a heavy pot, sweat onions, carrots, celery, and garlic.

Wash, peel, and dice sweet potatoes; add to sweated vegetables with ginger, peppers, curry, cilantro, basil, and thyme. Add stock; cook until potatoes are tender. Pass through a food mill and return to pot. Season with salt and pepper. If desired, to intensify flavor, add more herbs. Simmer 10 minutes.

To serve, ladle hot or cold soup into individual bowls. To each, add about 1 tablespoon yogurt and, if desired, 1 tablespoon cream. Cream should be heated if soup is served hot.

CHAPATI (UNLEAVENED BREAD FROM INDIA)
16 PORTIONS

INGREDIENTS

8 ounces whole-wheat flour
5 tablespoons (2½ fluid ounces) milk, warmed to just under 100°F
salt to taste
1 teaspoon olive oil
¼ cup (1 ounce) bread flour plus as needed for dusting

METHOD

Mix all ingredients (except bread flour for dusting) with a dough hook for 10 minutes. Let rest for 30 minutes in a warm place.

Cut dough into 16 equal pieces and knead into balls. On a marble slab, roll each ball until it is wafer-thin and about 3 to 4 inches in diameter, using bread flour for dusting.

Heat a griddle to at least 400°F; lightly oil griddle. Sauté each chapati for 30 seconds on each side. Remove and, with a paper towel, dry bread. Serve at once.

In India, chapati is served in place of rice and as a dipping medium for chutney and curries.

CANTONESE SWEET-AND-SOUR PORK
3 TO 6 PORTIONS

INGREDIENTS

1 pound boneless pork, cut in 1" cubes
¼ cup cornstarch
1 tablespoon soy sauce
¼ cup sugar
¼ cup white rice-wine vinegar
¾ cup water
oil as needed
½ teaspoon salt
½ teaspoon minced garlic
1 green bell pepper, cut in 1" squares
1 large carrot, sliced diagonally ¼" thick
½ cup canned pineapple chunks, drained
2 teaspoons cornstarch mixed with 2 tablespoons water

METHOD

Dredge pork in cornstarch. In a bowl, combine soy sauce, sugar, vinegar, and water.

Deep-fry pork in very hot oil (375°F) until cubes float. Drain well; place on serving dish.

Heat a wok or skillet over high heat until a drop of water immediately sizzles into steam. Add 2 tablespoons oil, salt, and garlic. Stir and cook until garlic is pungent. Add green pepper, carrot, and pineapple. Stir and cook 2 minutes, until colors of pepper and carrot have intensified but have not yet reached their peaks. Add soy mixture; stir and cook until boiling. Immediately stir in cornstarch-water mixture. Stir and cook until sauce has thickened. Pour over pork and serve.

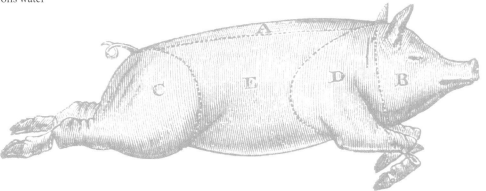

HONG KONG BARBECUED SHRIMP
4 PORTIONS

INGREDIENTS

2 pounds large headless raw shrimp
2 cloves garlic
½ teaspoon salt
½ cup soy sauce
½ cup lemon juice
3 tablespoons fresh parsley or cilantro, finely chopped
2 teaspoons minced green onions
½ teaspoon freshly ground black pepper
4 ounces diced jalapeño peppers
1 cup tomato salsa

METHOD

If shrimp are frozen, thaw. Shell and devein. Drain thoroughly and pat dry with paper towels. Arrange in shallow 1½-quart bowl.

In a small bowl, mash garlic with salt. Stir in soy sauce, lemon juice, parsley or cilantro, onions, black pepper, jalapenos, and salsa. Pour over shrimp. Cover and refrigerate for 1 hour.

Thread shrimp on 4 skewers. Grill 3 minutes, basting with marinade. Turn over. Grill 5 minutes longer, basting several times.

Serve on skewers. Bring marinade to a boil and serve as dipping sauce.

GRILLED EGGPLANT WITH APRICOT SAUCE (BEITINJAN BIL HAMOD)
6 TO 8 PORTIONS

INGREDIENTS
- 1 pound Italian (baby) eggplants
- 2 tablespoons olive oil
- 1 tablespoon minced garlic
- 1 teaspoon tarragon
- 1 teaspoon ground red pepper
- 2 tablespoons lemon juice
- 2 tablespoons orange juice
- 1 pint apricot preserves, heated until melted

METHOD

Wash and slice eggplant about 1/4" thick, leaving skin on.

Mix oil, garlic, tarragon, red pepper, and juices. Soak eggplant in marinade about 1 hour.

On a hot grill, cook eggplant 2 to 3 minutes, turning once. Cook briefly, as eggplant burns easily. Remove eggplant from grill. Brush with preserves; serve at once with additional preserves.

GRILLED VENISON MEDALLIONS
6 TO 8 PORTIONS

INGREDIENTS
- 1 pint olive oil
- 1 tablespoon minced fresh ginger
- ¼ cup diced onions, brunoise
- ¼ teaspoon red chili oil
- 2 tablespoons mango, peeled and diced
- 1 teaspoon black pepper
- 1 tablespoon fresh lemon juice
- 1 cinnamon stick
- 1 teaspoon chopped garlic in oil
- 2 pounds Cervena Denver leg of venison, cut in 3-ounce medallions

METHOD

Combine olive oil, ginger, onions, chili oil, mango, pepper, lemon juice, cinnamon stick, and garlic. Arrange venison in marinade. Cover; refrigerate at least 30 minutes or up to 1 hour.

Preheat grill. Remove venison from marinade, shaking well to remove excess oil. Grill to desired degree of doneness, preferably medium-rare.

Serve on chapati (recipe on page 31) with vindaloo sauce (recipe on page 33), chutney, and vegetables.

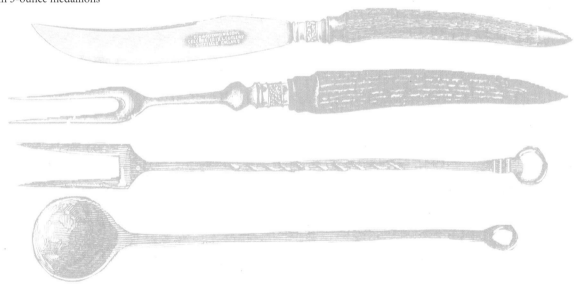

CHIPOLATA SAUSAGE
ABOUT 96 LINKS

INGREDIENTS
- 7½ pounds pork butts
- 1 pound pork fatback
- 1 tablespoon sage
- 1 teaspoon dried onion flakes
- 1 teaspoon thyme
- 1 teaspoon mace
- 1½ tablespoons salt
- 1 tablespoon ground black pepper
- 1 pint water
- 6 ounces unseasoned bread crumbs

METHOD

Remove and discard bones from pork butts. Grind pork and fatback through a ⅜" plate. Using a food processor, emulsify meats and refrigerate until very cold.

In an electric mixer, combine sage, onion, thyme, mace, salt, pepper, and water. Add crumbs. Refrigerate until very cold.

Combine meat and herb mixtures, mixing well. Using 28mm casings, stuff into 1" links. Wrap and refrigerate, or wrap and freeze.

Grill or bake sausages (if frozen, thaw in refrigerator before cooking) about 8 minutes, until internal temperature reaches 150°F, and serve at once.

VINDALOO (HOT CURRY) SAUCE
ABOUT 3 CUPS

INGREDIENTS

- 2 teaspoons roasted cumin
- 2 teaspoons roasted ground black mustard seeds
- 1 teaspoon roasted ground turmeric
- 1 teaspoon roasted ground black pepper
- 1 teaspoon ground cinnamon
- 1 teaspoon ground cardamom
- ½ teaspoon ground cloves
- ½ teaspoon ground nutmeg
- 1 tablespoon chopped fresh ginger
- 6 chopped red chiles
- ¼ cup olive or vegetable oil
- ⅔ cup diced onions
- ½ ounce chopped garlic in oil
- 1 cup cider vinegar
- 3 tablespoons brown sugar
- 1¼ cups chicken stock

METHOD

In blender, mix first 10 ingredients. Add 3 tablespoons oil and blend to a paste.

In remaining 1 tablespoon oil, sauté onions and garlic. Stir in spiced paste. Stir in vinegar and sugar; simmer about 5 minutes.

Add stock; cook until fat separates. Remove fat.

Vindaloo is sometimes sweetened with coconut milk and banana pulp. It also may be tightened with cornstarch slurry. It should be served in small portions as it is very spicy.

CINCINNATI SKILLET POTATOES
4 TO 6 PORTIONS

INGREDIENTS

- 1 pound old potatoes, peeled
- 4 tablespoons butter
- ½ cup Spanish onions, peeled and sliced
- ½ clove garlic, crushed
- 3 ounces fresh mushrooms, sliced
- 6 ounces smoked sausage, sliced ⅛" thick
- 1 teaspoon mustard
- 1 pint veal velouté sauce, heated (see note 1)
  salt as needed
  pepper as needed

METHOD

Steam potatoes until they are a little underdone. Slice and set aside.

Melt butter; add onions, garlic, and mushrooms. Sauté without allowing to color. Discard excess fat. Add sausage and heat through. Add potatoes.

Stir mustard into heated velouté; add to potato-sausage mixture. Season to taste with salt and pepper. Cook 3 minutes and serve.

Notes: 1. To prepare velouté, melt 4 tablespoons butter; blend in 4 tablespoons flour but do not brown; whisk in 2 cups veal stock and salt and pepper to taste; and cook, whisking constantly, until sauce is smooth and thickened. 2. To prepare recipe with new potatoes, cut potatoes into quarters after cooking. 3. To add an herb, choose cilantro for old potatoes, mint for new potatoes.

Variations: 1. Add 4 ounces of shredded cheddar cheese and brown in a hot (400°F) oven. 2. Substitute cooked diced chicken for sausage, and add 3 ounces of roasted bell peppers. 3. Substitute 8 ounces of sautéed vegetables for sausage.

CHOCOLATE GATEAU

TREASURER

George J. Pastor, Ed.D., CEC, CCE, AAC

Professor and Department Director

Tampa Bay Institute for Hospitality

and Culinary Studies

Hillsborough Community College

Tampa, FL

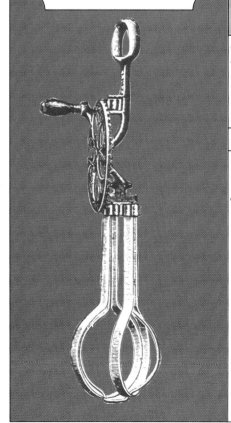

ELECTED NATIONAL OFFICERS 1997-1999

George J. Pastor
Ed.D., CEC, CCE, AAC

WHO THEY ARE, WHAT THEY DO BEST

Dr. Pastor earned his bachelor of arts degree at the University of Pittsburgh, his master's in public administration at Golden Gate University, and his doctorate in education at Nova-Southeastern University. He initiated the culinary arts and ACF cook-apprentice programs at Hillsborough Community College. And, as a culinary consultant, he has traveled extensively throughout the United States as well as to Canada, Moscow, Bogota, and Trinidad.

Since 1996, he has served as southeast region vice chair of the American Academy of Chefs. Since 1986, he has coached winning ACF junior and Vocational Industrial Clubs of America teams, as well as national and state gold and silver VICA winners. And, he has participated in many fund-raisers for his chapter, ACF Tampa Bay Chefs & Cooks Association, of which he is a founding member and past president. In addition to serving as current ACF national treasurer, Pastor sits on the ACF internal audit committee.

In 1991, when Superbowl XXV was played in Tampa, Pastor coordinated pre- and post-game meals for 14,000 VIP guests.

In January 1999, Pastor's ACF chapter paid tribute to his professional accomplishments by presenting him with its Lifetime Culinary Achievement Award.

VELVET PORK WITH CASHEWS

MY FINNISH WIFE'S CRACKERS
ABOUT 36

INGREDIENTS
½ cup unsalted butter
1 cup mashed potatoes (leftover or freshly made from fresh or instant potatoes)
1½ cups all-purpose flour

METHOD
In a saucepan, melt butter. Add potatoes, stirring constantly. Remove from heat.

Gradually beat in flour until a stiff dough is produced. Depending upon moistness and age of potatoes, pastry may not need all of the flour. Cover dough and set aside for 30 minutes.

On a lightly greased baking sheet, roll out dough as thin as possible. Bake at 375°F until lightly browned, about 10 minutes. Dough should have golden spots.

Remove from oven. While hot, with a pizza wheel or dough divider, cut into 3½" to 4" squares. Cool completely. Crackers become crisp as they cool. Store in an air-tight container.

BANANA-PEANUT SOUP
4 TO 6 PORTIONS

INGREDIENTS
6 tablespoons unsalted butter
1 medium onion, finely chopped
¼ cup unsifted flour
2 tablespoons curry powder mixed with 1 tablespoon flour (optional)
1 pound very ripe sweet bananas, peeled
2 tablespoons lemon juice
4 cups chicken or vegetable stock salt and pepper as needed
½ cup cream
½ cup crunchy peanut butter

METHOD
In a 3- to 4-quart pot, melt butter. Add onions; cover and sweat over low heat until onions are transparent. Whisk in flour. Whisk in curry mixture if using.

In food processor, purée bananas, lemon juice, and ½ cup stock. Stir into onion mixture. Whisk in remaining stock. Simmer for 15 minutes. Add salt and pepper to taste. Remove from heat.

Stir in cream and peanut butter. Heat through while stirring, then serve.

FISH FILLETS IN CITRUS SAUCE
4 PORTIONS

INGREDIENTS
- 1 teaspoon dried thyme
- ¼ teaspoon coarsely ground black pepper
- 1 tablespoon all-purpose flour
- 4 4-ounce fillets of any firm white fish (grouper, snapper, salmon, pompano, etc.)
- 2 tablespoons olive oil
- ½ cup fresh orange juice
- 1 tablespoon cider vinegar
- ½ cup orange marmalade
- 2 tablespoons unsalted butter

METHOD

Mix thyme, pepper, and flour; press into top (skinless) sides of fillets.

In a skillet over medium heat, heat oil. Arrange fillets in skillet, top sides down: cook about 2 minutes. Turn over; cook 2 minutes longer. Remove from pan.

Deglaze pan with orange juice; cook about 1 minute. Stir in vinegar and marmalade.

Return fish to pan. Cover and continue to cook 8 minutes or until done. Transfer fish to warm plates. Swirl butter into sauce; remove from heat (sauce will thicken slightly). Pour over fish and serve.

SIS LIPSON'S NASSAU GRITS
6 PORTIONS

INGREDIENTS
- 8 ounces sliced bacon
- 1 medium onion, finely chopped
- 1 medium green bell pepper, finely chopped
- ½ cup finely chopped cooked ham
- 5 medium, very ripe tomatoes, peeled, seeded, and chopped
- 1 cup white grits (regular, quick-cooking, or instant)

METHOD

In skillet, cook bacon until very crisp. Drain, crumble, and set aside.

Pour off all except 2 tablespoons bacon drippings. In reserved drippings, cook onion and pepper until onion is transparent. Stir in ham. Stir in tomatoes; cook at low heat for about 30 minutes.

In another pot, cook grits according to package directions. Stir in ham-tomato mixture. Serve very hot, each portion garnished with crumbled bacon.

VELVET PORK WITH CASHEWS
4 PORTIONS

INGREDIENTS
- ½ teaspoon sugar
- 1 teaspoon cornstarch
- 1½ tablespoons soy sauce
- 2 tablespoons rice wine
- 1 pound lean, boneless pork, cut into cubes
- 4 tablespoons peanut oil (or vegetable oil)
- ½ small can sliced water chestnuts, drained
- 1 medium onion, cut in small dice
- 2 cups fresh broccoli florets
- ½ cup unsalted cashew halves

METHOD

In a 1-quart bowl, mix sugar and cornstarch. Add soy sauce and wine; stir until sugar is dissolved. Add meat and toss. Set aside.

In a nonstick pan or wok, heat 2 tablespoons oil. Add water chestnuts, onion, and broccoli; stir-fry about 2 minutes. Remove vegetables from pan and keep warm.

Add remaining 2 tablespoons oil to pan. Add meat; stir-fry 4 to 5 minutes, until cooked. Return vegetables to pan. Add cashews; stir-fry 1 minute. Serve immediately, alone or over rice.

CURRIED CHICKEN BREASTS
4 TO 6 PORTIONS

INGREDIENTS
- 2 tablespoons olive oil
- 2 large onions, very finely chopped
- 2 large cloves garlic, peeled and crushed
- 1 teaspoon ground ginger
- 2 teaspoons chili powder
- 1 small chili pepper, minced (optional)
- 2 pounds boneless, skinless chicken breasts, cut in ¾" squares
- ½ cup seedless raisins
- 4 medium tomatoes, peeled, seeded, and chopped, or 14-ounce can chopped tomatoes
- 1 teaspoon lime juice
- 2 teaspoons turmeric
- 2 cups chicken or vegetable stock
- 1 stick cinnamon
- salt and pepper as needed

METHOD

In shallow 2-quart pan over medium heat, heat oil. Add onions and cook until transparent. Add garlic, ginger, chili powder, and chili pepper. Stir-fry for 1 minute.

Add chicken; cook until pieces are browned on all sides.

Add raisins, tomatoes, lime juice, turmeric, and stock; bring to a boil. Reduce heat, add cinnamon, cover pan, and simmer 1 hour. Add salt and pepper to taste and serve over steamed rice or couscous.

~ 70 Years of ~
PIONEERING AND PROFESSIONALISM

TWISTS OR SHELLS WITH NO-CREAM WHITE CLAM SAUCE
4 PORTIONS

INGREDIENTS

 1 tablespoon chopped shallots
½ cup olive oil
 1 tablespoon chopped garlic
¼ teaspoon chopped dried hot pepper
¼ cup dry white wine (e.g., dry sherry or dry vermouth)
 1 or 2 6-ounce cans chopped or minced clams, drained with juice reserved
 2 tablespoons chopped fresh parsley
 1 tablespoon butter
 2 tablespoons grated Parmesan cheese
   salt if needed
 8 ounces dried pasta, preferably twists or shells, cooked according to package directions

METHOD

In a small saucepan, sauté shallots in oil until translucent. Add garlic and hot pepper; stir and cook briefly. Add wine and reduce liquid by half. Add reserved clam juice and again reduce liquid by half. Stir in parsley, butter, clams, and cheese. Stir several times; turn off heat. Taste and add salt if needed. Pour over cooked pasta and serve.

Note: This very simple recipe can be altered easily to eliminate alcohol, cholesterol, and saturated fat.

CHOCOLATE GATEAU
4 TO 8 PORTIONS

INGREDIENTS

 6 ounces semisweet chocolate, broken into small pieces
 2 tablespoons coffee (Kahlúa, Tía Maria, etc.) or chocolate (crème de cacao, etc.) liqueur
½ cup unsalted butter, cut into small pieces
½ cup granulated sugar
 1 teaspoon vanilla extract
 3 egg yolks, beaten
   confectioners' sugar as needed
   fresh berries or poached pear halves

METHOD

In top of double-boiler, mix chocolate, liqueur, butter, sugar, and vanilla. In bottom of double-boiler, bring water to boil. Cover top and set over boiling water. Immediately turn off heat and allow to stand for 20 minutes.

Uncover top of double-boiler, remove it from bottom, blend ingredients well, and set aside to cool slightly. Stir in beaten yolks.

Pour into greased, floured 8" round cake pan. Bake at 325°F for about 20 minutes. Test for doneness by inserting toothpick in center of cake. Toothpick should come out slightly moist; do not dry out cake by overbaking.

Set cake, in pan, on a rack and cool 15 minutes. Remove from pan, return to rack, and allow to cool 2 hours before serving. Do not refrigerate before cutting as cold cake is difficult to cut. Dust each portion with sugar. Serve with berries or pears.

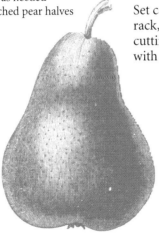

GRANNY SMITH APPLE GRANITÉ
APPROXIMATELY 1 QUART

INGREDIENTS

 2 cups apple juice
 1 cup granulated sugar
 2 tablespoons fresh lime juice
 1 tablespoon fresh lemon juice
 1 tablespoon fresh lime zest, chopped
 1 tablespoon fresh lemon zest, chopped
 1 Granny Smith apple, peeled and finely diced
½ teaspoon dried chopped mint leaves
   fresh fruit

METHOD

In a saucepan, combine apple juice and sugar. Bring to boil and stir until sugar is dissolved. Boil 1 minute. Set aside to cool.

Thoroughly mix remaining ingredients, except fresh fruit, with apple syrup. Pour into a shallow stainless steel pan. Place in freezer. Stir every 15 minutes until frozen yet granular in texture.

To serve, scrape each portion from surface of granité. Serve with fresh fruit.

CHAIRMAN,

AMERICAN ACADEMY OF CHEFS

Bert P. Cutino, CEC, AAC

Co-Owner, Sardine Factory

Monterey, CA

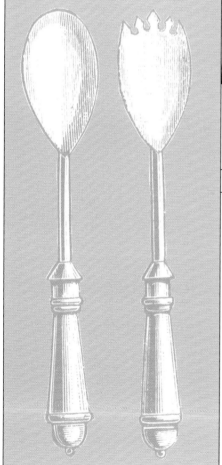

TORTELLINI WITH TOMATOES AND EGGPLANT CROUTONS

ELECTED NATIONAL OFFICERS 1997-1999

Bert P. Cutino
CEC, AAC

WHO THEY ARE, WHAT THEY DO BEST

*C*utino began his hospitality career at age 13. At 19, he was in charge of a restaurant and taking courses at Monterey Peninsula College; in 1954, he earned his degree. He holds the distinguished alumnus award (1982) from the California Association of Colleges and an honorary doctor of culinary arts (1988) from Johnson & Wales University. He also has been inducted into the California Tourism Hall of Fame (1997).

He is honorary chairman of the board of ACF Monterey Bay Chapter. He was ACF 1985-1989 western region vice president and 1988 ACF national Chef of the Year. He is a founding member of The Chef and the Child Foundation board and was finance chair for Horizons 2000 educational fund. He has been chairman of the American Academy of Chefs since 1995. ACF presented the Hermann G. Rusch Memorial Award to him in 1997. He has received the Antonin Carême medal (1987), two ACF President's Medallions, and the medal of honor of Les Amis d'Escoffier Society. He is a lifetime member and past commander-director of the Honorable Order of the Golden Toque, a trustee of the ACF Foundation, and a director of California Culinary Academy.

In a restored cannery workers' canteen, Cutino and his partner opened the nationally renowned Sardine Factory restaurant in 1968. They now own and operate 70 percent of Monterey's Cannery Row.

Cutino initiated Culinary Team USA West that competed at the 1988 international Culinary Olympics. His training program has helped the Sardine Factory succeed and aided former employees who opened restaurants. He organized continuing-education programs for local chefs, launched a culinary program at MPC, and was a visiting chef at Chef John Folse Culinary Institute of Nicholls State University.

He was first president of Les Toques Blanches/USA and has been inducted into its hall of fame and those of the California Restaurant Association and Distinguished Restaurants of North America. He has earned many gold medals and other culinary citations plus civic and community awards. He has appreared on regional and national television, sits on a number of boards, and works for many charitable organizations.

CRAB CAKES WITH SCAMPI-STYLE PRAWNS

ORANGE BISCOTTI
30 BISCUITS

INGREDIENTS
- 2 cups bleached all-purpose flour + additional for dusting
- 2 teaspoons baking powder
- pinch of salt
- ½ cup unsalted butter + plus additional for greasing pan
- 1 cup sugar
- 4 large eggs
- ⅓ cup curaçao
- zest of 2 oranges, finely minced

METHOD
Sift 2 cups flour, baking powder, and salt into a small bowl.

In another bowl, with an electric mixer, cream butter and sugar. Beat in eggs, 1 at a time. Beat in curaçao and zest. Stir in dry ingredients.

Immediately turn batter into a greased and floured 13" x 9" baking pan. Batter will be heavy; smooth and spread it evenly with a rubber spatula. Bake at 350°F for 20 minutes, until golden and a toothpick inserted in center comes out clean.

Remove pan from oven, but leave oven on. With cake still in pan, cut it on the diagonal into ¾"-wide strips. Then cut each strip in half. Let cool somewhat.

With a metal spatula or knife, coax strips from pan; set on wire rack until completely cool.

Spread strips on a baking sheet. Return to 350°F oven until toasted golden brown, turning once, for about 14 minutes. Cool completely on a wire rack.

To serve, stack biscotti crisscross on a small serving plate, 3 or 4 across. Store uncovered.

PRAWNS SAMBUCA
4 PORTIONS

INGREDIENTS

- ½ cup + 1 teaspoon olive oil
- 1 tablespoon chopped garlic
- 1 tablespoon chopped shallots
- 16 fresh Monterey Bay prawns, peeled and deveined
- 6 tablespoons chardonnay or other dry white wine
- ¼ cup sambuca
- ¼ cup fresh tomato, peeled and diced
- 1 tablespoon chopped fresh tarragon salt and pepper as needed
- ½ cup unsalted butter
- 2 quarts water
- 12 ounces raw dried angel hair pasta
- 4 fresh tarragon leaves

METHOD

In a skillet, heat ½ cup olive oil. Add garlic, shallots, and prawns. Cook 1 to 2 minutes. Add wine and sambuca. Heat and ignite. When flames die, add tomatoes, chopped tarragon, and salt and pepper to taste. Cook 2 minutes. Whisk in butter and reduce liquid by ⅓.

In a large pot, bring water to boil. Add a pinch of salt and remaining 1 teaspoon oil. Add pasta and cook 5 minutes (if using fresh pasta, cook only 3 minutes). Drain thoroughly.

On each plate, arrange ¼ of the pasta in center. Pour ¼ of sauce over pasta. Arrange 4 prawns on outer edge. Garnish with a tarragon leaf. Serve immediately.

TORTELLINI WITH TOMATOES, EGGPLANT CROUTONS AND BASIL-BALSAMIC VINAIGRETTE
6 PORTIONS

INGREDIENTS

- 2 pounds Roma tomatoes, washed and dried
  salt as needed
- 2 medium-sized eggplants
  water as needed
- 1½ tablespoons granulated garlic
  pepper as needed
  cooking oil as needed
- 2 teaspoons chopped fresh basil
- ½ cup vinegar
- 1 tablespoon Dijon mustard
- 2 tablespoons confectioners' sugar
- 1 tablespoon chopped shallots
- 1 teaspoon chopped garlic
- 1 cup olive oil
- 1 teaspoon salt and pepper mixed
- 1 pound tortellini filled with Gorgonzola cheese
- 2 tablespoons salad oil
  sprigs of Italian parsley

METHOD

Cut tomatoes in half lengthwise. Cut off blossom scars. Place on sheet pan, cut sides down. Sprinkle with 2 tablespoons salt. Bake at 350°F for 4 to 6 hours, until most of the juice has evaporated from the tomatoes.

Wash and trim eggplants; do not peel. Cut into ¼" cubes. Soak in salted water for 30 minutes. Drain and dry. Sprinkle with salt, pepper, and garlic. Deep-fry in cooking oil until golden brown. Drain well.

In a blender, process basil, vinegar, mustard, sugar, shallots, and garlic for 20 seconds. With motor on, gradually add olive oil, then mixed salt and pepper.

Cook tortellini in boiling salted water for 5 minutes. Drain; cool under running cold water and drain again. Toss with salad oil.

In a large bowl, toss tortellini with vinaigrette. Add tomatoes; toss again. Garnish with Italian parsley and eggplant croutons. Serve immediately at room temperature.

SALMON ROSES WITH MONTEREY SPOT PRAWNS
4 PORTIONS

INGREDIENTS

4 salmon bellies
   salt and pepper as needed
1 quart court bouillon or chicken stock
   unsalted butter as needed
⅓ cup shallots, chopped
⅓ cup onion, chopped
1 cup (8 fluid ounces) champagne
1 cup champagne vinegar
⅓ cup dry vermouth
1 cup heavy cream
2 cups fine cracker meal
2 tablespoons granulated garlic
½ cup fresh basil chiffonade
12 large (16/20 count) prawns, peeled and
   deveined
⅔ cup vegetable oil
1 teaspoon olive oil
2 cups (packed) fresh spinach, washed,
   drained, and stems removed
1 medium potato

METHOD

Fillet salmon, removing pin bones. Each fillet should weigh about 4 ounces. Slice bellies into strips 12" x 1". Pound each strip and season with salt and pepper. Roll each strip tightly into a circle in the shape of a rose, securing each with a toothpick. Poach in court boullon for 5 minutes.

In a little butter, sauté shallots and onions. Deglaze pan with champagne, vinegar, and vermouth. Reduce liquid by ½. Add cream and again reduce by ½. Whisk in 1 cup butter until emulsified. Add salt and pepper to taste.

Thoroughly blend cracker meal, garlic, basil chiffonade, and 2½ table spoons of mixed salt and pepper. Dredge prawns in mixture. Fry in ⅓ cup vegetable oil until golden brown. Remove from oil, drain, and keep warm.

In olive oil in a hot skillet, cook spinach for 15 seconds. Keep warm.

Peel potato; cut into 12 lengthwise slices, ⅛" thick. In remaining ⅓ cup vegetable oil, pan-fry potato slices until they are as crisp as potato chips.

Per portion, place ½ cup spinach in center of plate. Top with a slamon rose. Arrange butter sauce around salmon and spinach. Arrange 3 prawns on one side and three potato chips to the back of the salmon on the other side.

CRAB CAKES WITH SCAMPI-STYLE PRAWNS
6 PORTIONS

INGREDIENTS

1 pound Dungeness crab meat, well-drained
¼ cup finely chopped red bell pepper
¼ cup finely diced chives
1 cup mashed potato
1 whole egg, slightly beaten
   salt as needed
¼ teaspoon black pepper
¼ teaspoon Tabasco sauce
¼ teaspoon Worcestershire sauce
1 cup fresh bread crumbs
   olive oil as needed
1 tablespoon chopped garlic
1 tablespoon chopped shallots
¼ cup chopped fresh mushrooms
¼ cup chopped peeled tomatoes
¼ cup chopped scallion
¼ cup dry white wine
1 cup lobster stock or clam broth
½ cup heavy cream
2 tablespoons softened butter
¼ cup chopped fresh parsley
⅓ teaspoon ground white pepper
18 large (16/20 count) Monterey prawns,
   heads removed and split lengthwise
2 pounds Swiss chard, washed thoroughly,
   drained, and blanched
2 tablespoons finely diced tomato
2 tablespoons finely minced fresh parsley

METHOD

Lightly combine crab, bell pepper, chives, mashed potato, egg, dash of salt, black pepper, and Tabasco and Worcestershire sauces. Divide mixture into 6 equal portions. Shape each into a patty. Coat with crumbs. Heat a griddle at medium. Add a little oil. Sauté crab cakes approximately 4 minutes on each side, until golden brown. Remove from pan; keep warm.

In a saucepan, heat 2 tablespoons olive oil. Add garlic and shallots; sauté 1 minute. Add mushrooms, chopped tomato, and scallion; sauté 1 minute. Deglaze pan with wine; cook 2 minutes. Add stock; bring to a boil. Add cream; bring to a boil again. Lower heat; reduce liquid to 1½ cups, stirring occasionally. Whisk in softened butter and parsley. Season with salt to taste and white pepper. Keep warm.

In a large skillet, heat ½ cup olive oil. Add prawns; sauté briefly. Add sauce and reduce.

In a medium skillet, heat ½ cup olive oil. Add chard and salt and pepper to taste. Heat.

To serve, on each warm dinner plate, arrange a bed of about ½ cup chard. Set a crab cake on chard. Garnish with finely diced tomato and parsley. Surround with three prawns. Pour sauce over prawns. Serve at once.

MARINATED LAMB CHOPS WITH BAROLO SAUCE
4 PORTIONS

INGREDIENTS
6¼ cups + 1 tablespoon olive oil
2 tablespoons lemon thyme
¾ cup garlic, chopped
2 tablespoons rosemary, chopped
½ cup Dijon mustard
  salt as needed
  cracked pepper as needed
  juice of 4 lemons
  4- to 6-bone lamb rack, frenched, silver
    skin removed, and cut into 2-bone chops
¼ cup shallots, chopped
¼ cup carrot, finely diced
1 medium onion, chopped
2 stalks celery, diced
1 shiitake mushroom, cleaned and chopped
½ cup tomato, peeled and chopped
4 cups Barolo
½ cup orange juice
½ cup grapefruit juice
1 quart lamb stock
1 medium sweet onion, sliced ¼" thick,
    tossed in herbed flour, and fried crisp
4 cups mashed potatoes
  steamed baby vegetables

METHOD
In a large bowl, mix 6¼ cups olive oil, lemon thyme, ½ cup garlic, rosemary, mustard, ¼ cup salt, ¼ cup cracked pepper, and lemon juice. Add lamb chops. Refrigerate and let marinate for 4 hours.

In a hot skillet, sear chops on both sides. Finish cooking in 400°F oven for 10 minutes, until internal temperature reaches 130°F.

In a heavy-bottomed saucepan, heat remaining 1 tablespoon oil until it begins to smoke. Add shallots, remaining ¼ cup garlic, carrot, onion, celery, and mushroom; sauté until caramelized. Add tomato and cook out all liquid. Add Barolo and citrus juices; reduce by ½. Add stock; again reduce by ½. Add 1 tablespoon mixed salt and pepper.

Remove chops from oven; let rest 1 minute. Cut each in half. On each plate, arrange 4 chops in a circle, with bones sticking straight up. Top bones with onion rings. Arrange sauce around chops. Accompany with mashed potatoes and steamed baby vegetables.

SEARED GREEN BEANS, TOMATOES, AND POTATOES SICILINI-STYLE
6 PORTIONS

INGREDIENTS
3 pounds small red-skinned new potatoes,
    each about the size of a small lime
  sea salt as needed
  water as needed
⅓ cup extra-virgin olive oil
  freshly ground black pepper
2 pounds flat Italian or rounded Blue Lake
    green beans
1 large red onion, halved and thinly sliced
½ cup red-wine vinegar
3 medium-size Roma tomatoes

METHOD
Scrub potatoes. Bring to boil in salted water. Cover. Cook until potatoes offer little resistance when pierced with a fork, 20 to 30 minutes. Remove from heat; run cold water into pot to stop the cooking. Drain well. When cool enough to handle, remove skins. Put in serving bowl. Add salt and olive oil, then toss. Sprinkle with a few grindings of pepper.

Clean and snap off ends of beans. In a steamer, bring water to a boil. Place beans in basket and steam until tender, about 8 to 10 minutes. Drain.

Separate onion into half-rings; put in a large serving bowl. Stir in vinegar, then beans. Toss in potatoes. Season to taste with salt and pepper.

Wash tomatoes well. Cut in halves. Arrange potato-bean-onion mixture on each plate. Garnish with a tomato half.

Serve at room temperature.

~ 70 Years of ~
PIONEERING AND PROFESSIONALISM

OSSO BUCO CANNERY ROW
4 PORTIONS

INGREDIENTS
- 1 cup cooking oil
- 4 veal shanks, each 4" high or about 2½ pounds
  flour as needed
- 4 onions, peeled and chopped
- 2 large carrots, peeled and chopped
- 4 stalks celery, chopped
- 4 tomatoes, peeled, seeded, and diced
- ¼ cup chopped fresh basil
- 2 teaspoons chopped fresh thyme
- 4 bay leaves
- 2 cups dry white wine
- 2 cups orange juice
- 2 quarts veal or beef stock
- 1½ teaspoons salt
- ½ teaspoon ground black pepper
- 2 oranges, washed and cut in quarters
- 4 fresh thyme leaves

METHOD
In a large pot, heat oil. Dredge veal in flour; add to pot and brown on all sides. Remove meat from pot; set aside.

To same pot, add onions, carrots, celery, and tomatoes; sauté 1 minute. Add basil, thyme, bay leaves, wine, orange juice, and stock. Return shanks to pot. Season with salt and pepper. Add orange quarters. Cover. Set pot in 400°F oven for approximately 3½ hours. After 3 hours, check to see if veal is done. A knife should insert easily into the shank, or a meat thermometer should register well-done.

Remove shanks and oranges from pot. Purée vegetables and liquid in food processer. Return to pot; bring to boil. Return shanks to pot; heat through.

For each portion, serve a shank with soft polenta, rice, or pasta, surrounded with vegetables and sauce. Place a thyme leaf on each shank.

FRIED ARTICHOKES
6 PORTIONS

INGREDIENTS
  cold water as needed
- 4 lemons
- 12 baby artichokes, each about 3" long
- 2 large eggs
- 2 tablespoons milk
- 1 cup all-purpose flour
- 1½ cups unseasoned fine dry bread crumbs
- 2 tablespoons finely minced garlic
- 2 quarts olive oil
  sea salt

METHOD
Pour water into a large bowl. Extract juice from 1 lemon; add to water. Keep a second lemon handy for passing a knife through it as you trim artichokes (to prevent knife blade from turning black).

Working with 1 artichoke at a time, cut off ½" from top. Remove outer leaves, stopping where leaves are thin and pale green. Cut off and discard stem. Cut artichoke in half and place in lemon water. Repeat until all artichokes are in lemon water. Extract juice from lemon used to clean knife blade, and add it and its rind to lemon water. Let artichokes soak 15 minutes.

Almost fill a large pot with water; add juice and rinds of remaining 2 lemons. Bring to boil. Drain artichokes; add to pot. Cover; cook 10 minutes, until firm. Drain and rinse under cold running water; drain again.

Cover work surface with waxed paper. In shallow bowl, beat eggs and milk. Put flour in a deep bowl. Mix crumbs and garlic in another deep bowl.

Dust each artichoke with flour, coat with egg wash letting excess drip off, and dredge in garlic crumbs, making sure artichokes are coated completely. Place on waxed paper.

Pour oil into a 6-quart pot to a depth of about 2". Heat at medium to 350°F. Test by dropping in a cube of bread, which should brown quickly but not burn.

In two or three batches, gently lower artichokes into deep-fat. Fry until a rich golden brown, approximately 4 minutes. With a slotted spoon, remove to brown paper or paper towels to drain. Keep warm in a 300°F oven, uncovered, until all have been cooked.

Serve hot with sea salt.

SECRETARY/TREASURER,

AMERICAN ACADEMY OF CHEFS

Fritz Sonnenschmidt, CMC, AAC

Culinary Dean

The Culinary Institute of America

Hyde Park, NY

VEGETARIAN BORSCHT

ELECTED NATIONAL OFFICERS 1997-1999

Fritz Sonnenschmidt
CMC, AAC

WHO THEY ARE, WHAT THEY DO BEST

A member of ACF for 35 years, Sonnenschmidt has served as president of his chapter, ACF Mid-Hudson Culinary Association. In addition to his position at the CIA, he is a culinary lecturer, a certified ACF and WACS culinary judge, and chair of the national certification committee of ACF. In 1994, he was named ACF national Chef of the Year.

Among Sonnenschmidt's many awards are the 1973 Escoffier chair for culinary excellence, the Geneva Gold Medal, the Jerusalem gold medal for culinary excellence in Jewish cooking, and the Otto Gentch gold medal. In 1983, he earned designation as an ACF-certified master chef.

As a member of 1976 Culinary Team USA, Sonnenschmidt competed in that year's international Culinary Olympics in Frankfurt, Germany, and won two individual gold medals. At the 1984 Culinary Olympics, he served as captain of the New York regional team that earned two gold medals and grand prize in silver. And, at the 1988 Culinary Olympics, he again captained the New York regional team, which was awarded the grand prize in gold.

Sonnenschmidt is a member of the Order of the Golden Toque, International Chefs Association, Chefs de Cuisine of America, Verband der Koche Deutschland (German Cooks Association), and Chaine de Rotisseur of Les Amis de Escoffier.

He attended culinary school in his native Germany, then worked as a chef in restaurants in Munich and in London before emigrating to New York in 1962. Before joining the CIA in 1968, he was executive chef at Eldorado Shore and Yacht Club, New Rochelle, and at Sheraton Hotels in Manhattan.

Three of Sonnenschmidt's books have been published: *The Professional Chef's Art of Garde Manger*, now in its sixth edition; *Dining with Sherlock Holmes*, and *Sherlock Holmes at the CIA*.

GRILLED MARINATED
CHICKEN BREASTS WITH
ORANGE-BALSAMIC JUS

CARPACCIO OF RADISHES
4 PORTIONS

INGREDIENTS
1 small clove garlic
    coarse salt to taste
2 tablespoons cider vinegar
    zest of ½ lemon, grated
½ teaspoon (or to taste) honey
½ pound daikons (large Asian radishes)
    small piece gingerroot, about ½" thick,
        shredded
1 tablespoon toasted sunflower seeds
2 tablespoons hazelnut oil
    toast as needed

METHOD
With the flat side of a knife blade, mash garlic with salt. In a saucepan, combine with vinegar, lemon zest, and honey. Bring to boil over medium heat; keep warm.

Wash and peel daikons. With a knife or mandoline, slice thinly.

Place daikons on serving plate; pour hot marinade over them. Sprinkle with ginger and sunflower seeds. Drizzle with oil. Serve with toast.

VEGETARIAN BORSCHT
4 PORTIONS

INGREDIENTS
1 bay leaf
1 sprig fresh thyme or 1½ teaspoons dried
1 clove garlic
4 tablespoons butter, margarine, or
    vegetable oil
2 medium red onions, finely diced
1 small head savoy cabbage, shredded
1 or 2 carrots, peeled and shredded
2 quarts vegetable stock
2 red beets, medium to large, peeled
    salt as needed
    sugar as needed
    vinegar as needed
    garlic croutons as needed
1 cup sour cream
4 hot whole boiled potatoes (optional)

METHOD
On a square of cheese cloth folded in several layers, place bay leaf, thyme, and garlic. Gather up edges of cloth; tie with string to form a sachet or pouch.

In a soup pot, heat butter. Add onions; sauté until transparent. Add cabbage and carrots; sauté for 5 minutes. Add stock, beets, and sachet; simmer for 1 to 1½ hours. Remove and discard sachet. Remove beets, shred, and return to pot. Season with salt, sugar, and vinegar.

To serve hot, garnish each portion with garlic croutons. Pass sour cream separately.

To serve cold, mix sour cream into soup. Drop one hot potato into each portion.

STIR-FRIED DUCKLING IN PINOT NOIR SAUCE
15 PORTIONS

INGREDIENTS

2 cups minced shallots
1 quart Pinot Noir
1 quart veal or chicken stock
   salt and pepper as needed
5 pounds boneless, skinless duck
   cornstarch as needed
1 cup peanut oil
1½ pounds fresh mushrooms, thickly sliced
3 tablespoons minced ginger
1 tablespoon minced garlic

METHOD

Bring shallots and Pinot Noir to boil; reduce by ⅔. Add stock. Simmer 10 minutes. Season to taste with salt and pepper. Reserve sauce.

Julienne duck meat. Mix with cornstarch, peanut oil, and salt and pepper to taste. Stir-fry duck. Add mushrooms, ginger, and garlic and cook 5 minutes. Add sauce, mix well, and heat through.

BRAISED CURLY ENDIVE WITH MILLET CAKES AND DILL SAUCE
4 PORTIONS

INGREDIENTS

¾ cup millet
1 cup milk, heated to lukewarm
   salt as needed
1 to 2 tablespoons flour
1 whole egg
1 egg white
¼ cup sunflower oil
2 heads curly endive
   water as needed
1 tablespoon vegetable oil
2 tablespoons butter or margarine
¼ cup diced onion
1 carrot, peeled and diced
¼ cup diced leeks
¼ cup celery, peeled and diced
   pepper as needed
   Parmesan cheese as needed
1 cup cottage cheese
2 cups vegetable stock
   juice of ½ lemon
3 to 4 tablespoons finely chopped fresh dill

METHOD

In a bowl, combine millet, milk, and salt to taste. Bring to boil. Simmer 5 minutes. Cool. Add flour, egg, and egg white.

In a small skillet, heat a little sunflower oil. Ladle a little batter into pan. Fry, turning once, until golden brown on both sides. Keep warm. Repeat, using all batter and sunflower oil.

Cut endives in halves. Rinse well. Blanch in boiling salted water for 3 minutes; drain and shock in ice water. Remove and discard cores.

In a skillet, heat vegetable oil and 1 tablespoon butter or margarine. Add onions, carrots, leeks, and celery; sweat for 2 to 3 minutes.

With remaining 1 tablespoon butter, grease an ovenproof dish. Place endives in dish, cut sides down. Spread sweated vegetables over endives. Season with salt and pepper, cover, and bake at 350°F for 20 to 30 minutes. Sprinkle with Parmesan; bake uncovered until cheese is browned.

In a saucepan, heat cottage cheese and stock until warmed through; do not boil. Season with lemon juice, dill, and salt and pepper to taste. Keep warm.

To serve, arrange curly endive on each plate, top with a millet cake, and serve with dill sauce.

GRILLED MARINATED CHICKEN BREASTS WITH ORANGE-BALSAMIC JUS
4 PORTIONS

INGREDIENTS

1 to 2 sprigs fresh thyme
½ cup orange juice
3 tablespoons olive oil
   salt as needed
   freshly ground pepper as needed
4 boneless chicken breasts
3 tablespoons finely diced shallots
¼ cup balsamic vinegar

METHOD

Combine thyme, orange juice, 2 tablespoons oil, and salt and pepper to taste. Add chicken. Cover and refrigerate at least 2 hours or overnight.

Drain chicken, reserving marinade. Arrange chicken on a grill over medium heat. Grill 20 minutes, turning several times. Remove; let stand 5 minutes.

In a skillet, heat remaining 1 tablespoon oil. Add shallots and sauté until golden brown. Add reserved marinade and vinegar; reduce to consistency of syrup. Season with salt and pepper. Serve chicken and jus with red-wine risotto (recipe below).

RED-WINE RISOTTO
4 PORTIONS

INGREDIENTS

3 tablespoons olive oil
3 tablespoons chopped shallots
5 ounces Arborio rice
1¾ to 2 cups chicken stock, boiling
¼ cup dry red wine
1 to 2 tablespoons grated Parmesan cheese
2 tablespoons cold butter
   salt and pepper as needed

METHOD

In medium-sized saucepan, heat oil. Add shallots and sauté until transparent. Stir in rice, coating with oil and mixing with shallots. Add stock and red wine. Stir and cook over medium heat until creamy, approximately 15 to 20 minutes. Let rest 5 minutes. Stir in cheese, butter, and salt and pepper to taste. Serve at once.

TURKEY CUTLETS WITH MAPLE-BRANDY SAUCE
6 PORTIONS

INGREDIENTS
olive oil as needed
1 cup finely chopped Vidalia onions
5 tablespoons finely chopped garlic
1 cup ketchup
½ cup maple syrup
½ cup balsamic vinegar
¾ cup brandy
salt as needed
ground black pepper as needed
1 cup horseradish
2 tablespoons ground cumin
1 tablespoon paprika
1 teaspoon crushed pink peppercorns
2 tablespoons kosher salt
12 4-ounce turkey cutlets

METHOD
In a saucepan, heat 2 tablespoons oil. Sauté onions and 2 tablespoons garlic. Stir in ketchup, syrup, vinegar, and brandy. Simmer 20 to 25 minutes. Add salt and pepper if needed.

Combine horseradish, cumin, remaining 3 tablespoons garlic, paprika, 1 teaspoon ground black pepper, crushed pink peppercorns, and kosher salt in a mortar. With a pestle, pound mixture to a paste. Rub lightly into cutlets. Spray with oil. Sauté 2 to 3 minutes on each side.

Serve cutlets with maple-brandy sauce, accompanied by sautéed romaine (recipe below).

SAUTÉED ROMAINE
6 PORTIONS

INGREDIENTS
2 tablespoons grated fresh ginger
1 cup light soy sauce
¼ cup dry white wine
2 heaping tablespoons brown sugar
3 tablespoons sesame oil
3 heads of romaine, washed, drained, dried, and cut in half lengthwise

METHOD
In a blender or food processor, semi-emulsify ginger, soy sauce, wine, brown sugar, and sesame oil. Brush romaine leaves with marinade.

In a skillet that has been sprayed with sesame oil, sauté romaine for 3 to 5 minutes. Remove from pan and serve at once or keep warm.

Note: If marinade is boiled, cooled, covered, and refrigerated, it can be used as marinade for spare ribs, with or without barbecue sauce.

MODERNIZED HASENPFEFFER
1 PORTION

INGREDIENTS
olive oil as needed
6 ounces shredded raw rabbit
1 tablespoon red onion, finely diced
⅓ cup apple wine
2 tablespoons ketchup
½ teaspoon cornstarch
1 cup rabbit stock or light beer
½ teaspoon red currant jelly
⅓ teaspoon fresh thyme, minced
2 ounces tofu, cubed
ground black pepper as needed
salt as needed
1 teaspoon fresh parsley, minced
1 teaspoon whipped cream or nonfat yogurt
½ cup shredded savoy cabbage
¼ cup julienned potatoes
⅓ cup water
1 teaspoon chopped chives
½ teaspoon frozen apple juice concentrate
⅓ teaspoon caraway seeds

METHOD
In a skillet, heat 1 tablespoon oil. Sear rabbit; remove and set aside.

Add a little more oil to pan. Add onions; sauté until transparent. Add wine and reduce completely. Add ketchup and brown. Add cornstarch, stock or beer, jelly, and thyme; bring to boil. Add tofu; simmer 5 minutes. Add rabbit, lots of black pepper, and salt to taste. Heat through. Fold in parsley and whipped cream or yogurt. Keep warm.

In a skillet in 1 tablespoon oil, stir-fry cabbage and potatoes. Add water and steam until potatoes are cooked through. Add chives, salt and pepper to taste, apple juice concentrate, and caraway seeds. Serve with rabbit.

VICE PRESIDENT,

CENTRAL REGION

Michel D. Bouit, CEC, AAC

President

Michel Bouit International, Inc.

Chicago, IL

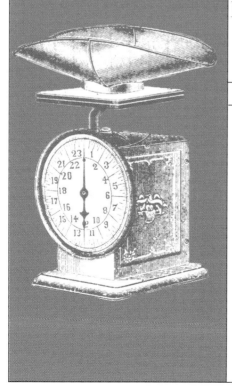

BREAST OF DUCK ROUENNAIS

ELECTED NATIONAL OFFICERS 1997-1999

Michel D. Bouit
CEC, AAC

WHO THEY ARE, WHAT THEY DO BEST

*B*ouit, a French-born American, owns and serves as president of a culinary consulting company that coordinates the American Culinary Classic, Pierre Tattinger Competition, Bocuse d'Or, and National Game Fish Cookoff. His expertise results from education, training, and culinary work in Europe and the United States, including 29 years as executive chef and director of dining services for an international bank.

A member of ACF Chicago Chefs of Cuisine, Inc., he was named ACF national Chef of the Year in 1989. He also belongs to The World Association of Cooks Societies, Le Vatel Club du Midwest, Societé Culinaire Philanthropique, Les Amis d'Escoffier, and Disciples de Maître Paul Bocuse. He is executive director of the American Bocuse d'Or Academy, The Bocuse d'Or USA Foncours and The Auguste Escoffier USA Grand Prix, and USA director of Euro-Toques.

~ *70 Years of* ~
PIONEERING AND PROFESSIONALISM

Bouit's company specializes in creating international culinary events and competitions—e.g., The Chefs' Triathlon—plus worldwide culinary travel and an educational program, Cooking with the Masters, in France.

In addition to earning a gold medal in 1976 and a silver in 1980 at the international Culinary Olympics in Frankfurt, Germany, Bouit has received a number of other awards including his chapter's 1980 Chef of the Year, a 1986 ACF President's Medallion, life membership in his chapter, 1989 ACF Mr. Communicator, ACF honorary life membership, and Les Amis d'Escoffier Society life membership. In his nine years as ACF vice president, his central region was Region of the Year three times.

Bouit has served on the ACF national culinary committee since 1987. He was 1993-1994 ACF national secretary/treasurer, 1991-1993 central-region chairman of the board, and 1986-1987 chapter president. He is also active in the National Restaurant Association; he was 1991 American Culinary Classic chair, 1987 advisor/regional coordinator, and 1986-1991 Chicago culinary-arts salon advisor/regional coordinator.

LEMON TART
WITH LAVENDER FLOWERS

SQUASH AND MUSSEL SOUP
4 PORTIONS

INGREDIENTS

- 2 quarts mussels, scrubbed and beards removed
- 1 teaspoon fennel seeds
- ¼ cup dry white wine
- 2 tablespoons butter
- 1 large sweet onion, finely sliced
- 4 cloves garlic, peeled and crushed
- 2 pounds yellow squash, peeled, seeded, and diced
- 4 cups boiling water
  salt and pepper as needed
- ½ cup heavy cream

METHOD

In a large covered pot over high heat, cook mussels, fennel seeds, and wine for 3 to 4 minutes. Remove from heat as soon as most mussels have opened. Strain liquid through cheesecloth; reserve. Remove mussels from shells.

In a heavy saucepan over low heat, melt butter; add onion and sweat until transparent. Add garlic and squash; continue cooking until squash begins to disintegrate.

In another saucepan, bring reserved mussel liquid to boil. Add to squash with boiling water. Boil gently, lid ajar, about 30 minutes. Pass through a food mill. Season to taste with salt and pepper. Return to boiling. Stir in mussels and cream. Heat through.

FILET OF BEEF WITH FRICASSÉE OF ARTICHOKES AND PEPPERS
4 PORTIONS

INGREDIENTS

- 4 fresh artichoke hearts
- ½ sweet green pepper, cut in small dice
- ½ sweet red pepper, cut in small dice
  butter as needed
- 2 cups beef consommé
- 4 plum tomatoes, peeled and diced
- ¼ cup olive oil
  juice of one lime
  salt and pepper as needed
- 4 6-ounce filets of beef
- 1 lime, quartered

METHOD

Sauté artichokes and peppers in a little butter; reserve. Reduce consommé by ⅓. Sauté tomatoes in a little butter; reserve.

Whisk oil and reduced consommé to an emulsion. Add vegetables and lime juice; season to taste with salt and pepper.

Grill filets. Top each with a lime quarter and serve surrounded with vegetables.

STUFFED BAKED FISH
4 PORTIONS

INGREDIENTS
4 ounces fish liver
  salted water as needed
2 ounces (2-3 standard slices) crustless,
  day-old bread
  milk as needed
2 tablespoons butter
1 small onion, finely chopped
1 clove garlic, finely chopped
  handful young sorrel leaves, finely shredded
  pinch fennel seeds, pounded to powder in
   a mortar
½ teaspoon fresh savory, finely chopped
1 hard-cooked egg, shelled and quartered
1 raw egg
  2-pound whole red snapper or other fish,
   gutted, scaled, and head removed
  salt and pepper as needed
  olive oil as needed
  fresh or dried wild fennel as needed
½ cup Muscadet or Sauvignon Blanc
1 lemon, sliced
  dried unseasoned bread crumbs as needed
1 tablespoon butter

METHOD
Poach liver in salted water to cover for 1 minute, until firm but still pink. Cut into small pieces. Soak bread in milk to cover; lightly squeeze out milk.

In fry pan, melt 1 tablespoon butter; add onion and garlic and cook over low heat until softened and lightly colored. Add sorrel; cook until wilted. In food processor, process contents of fry pan, fennel seeds, savory, liver, bread, hard-cooked egg, and raw egg to a coarse purée.

Season fish with salt and pepper. Spoon stuffing into cavity; secure with skewers or kitchen string. Rub fish with 1 tablespoon olive oil. Place in long gratin pan. Surround with fennel stalks. Add wine and lemon slices. Sprinkle with crumbs. Drizzle with olive oil. Bake at 400°F for 40 minutes, basting several times. Dot with remaining 1 tablespoon butter and serve in baking pan.

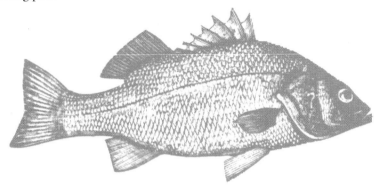

TOURNEDOS OF SCALLOPS
4 PORTIONS

INGREDIENTS
2 shallots
½ cup dry white wine
  coarsely ground pepper as needed
1 bouquet garni
2 pounds mussels in shells, beards
   removed and thoroughly scrubbed
½ cup cream
6 tablespoons butter
1 large celeriac, peeled and diced
20 large sea scallops
4 strips bacon
8 ounces morels, cleaned

METHOD
Place shallots, wine, pepper, and bouquet garni in a casserole. Bring to boil. Add mussels; cover and cook until mussels open. Strain liquid through cheesecloth and reserve. Remove mussels from shells; reserve 4 for garniture. Return remaining mussels to casserole; add cream. Simmer a few minutes; add 4 tablespoons butter. Keep warm.

Cook celeriac in reserved mussel liquid. Drain and purée. Keep warm.

For each portion, cluster 5 scallops together in the shape of a round; wrap a slice of bacon around each and secure with a toothpick. Sear in a greased skillet; finish cooking in a 350°F oven for 5 minutes or until done.

Sauté morels in remaining 2 tablespoons butter.

Serve tournedos with mussel sauce, each portion garnished with a reserved mussel and accompanied by celeriac purée garnished with morrels.

PISSALADIÈRE WITH RED SNAPPER
4 PORTIONS

INGREDIENTS
14 ounces Vidalia onions, finely sliced
  olive oil as needed
4 cloves garlic, minced
  salt and pepper as needed
2 ounces kalamata or niçoise olives, pitted
  and chopped
4 anchovy fillets
  fresh thyme, minced, to taste
8 4-ounce red snapper fillets

METHOD
Sauté onions in a little olive oil; add garlic, then salt and pepper to taste. Cook 35 minutes over low heat, stirring frequently.

Remove from heat. Add olives, anchovies, and thyme. Spread in a shallow tart pan. Top with red snapper. Season with salt and pepper. Bake at 350°F for 10 minutes.

Serve warm with seasoned salad greens and minced fresh chives.

BREAST OF DUCK ROUENNAIS
4 PORTIONS

INGREDIENTS
1 pound duck breasts, skin removed and reserved
5 tablespoons kosher salt
5 tablespoons sugar
  crushed thyme to taste
  crushed bay leaf to taste
  olive oil as needed
¼ cup cider vinegar
12 ounces mesclun
  salt and freshly ground pepper as needed
1 Granny Smith apple, diced
2 ounces Edam cheese, coarsely shredded

METHOD
To cure duck like gravlax, rub breasts with mixture of salt, sugar, thyme, and bay leaf. In nonmetallic bowl, refrigerate for 1 day. Rinse breasts and dry. Coat with olive oil, cover with plastic wrap, and refrigerate for 1 additional day.

Dice duck skin. In skillet, dry slowly over low heat like lardons.

Whisk ¾ cup olive oil with vinegar. Season mesclun to taste with salt and pepper. Toss with vinaigrette.

Place mesclun in center of each plate. Thinly slice duck and arrange on greens. Garnish with apple, duck lardons, cheese, and freshly ground pepper.

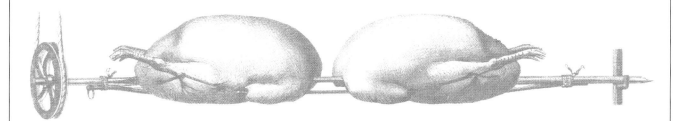

PHEASANT WITH APPLES
4 PORTIONS

INGREDIENTS
1 large onion, thinly sliced
  corn or peanut oil as needed
  2- to 2½-pound pheasant, cleaned and cut into serving pieces
3 large Rome Beauty apples, cored, quartered, and cut in 3/4" slices
1 tablespoon lemon zest, julienned
1 tablespoon raisins
1 bay leaf
1 whole clove
  salt as needed
  freshly ground black pepper as needed
¼ cup unsweetened applesauce
1 cup brown chicken stock

METHOD
In a large heavy saucepan, sauté onion in a little oil until golden brown.

In a heavy skillet in ¼ cup oil, cook pheasant pieces until very brown, at least 5 minutes on each side. Drain on paper towels; add to onion in saucepan. Add apples and zest; cook until apples are soft, about 5 minutes. Add raisins, bay leaf, clove, salt and pepper to taste, applesauce, and chicken stock. Cover and cook 20 minutes. Reduce heat to medium, uncover, and cook 40 to 45 minutes until done.

LEMON TART WITH LAVENDER FLOWERS
4 PORTIONS

INGREDIENTS

1 sheet frozen puff pastry
5 large eggs, lightly beaten
1 cup + 6 tablespoons granulated sugar
   zest of ½ lemon, grated
   juice of 4 lemons
1 cup unsalted butter
2 tablespoons dried organic lavender flowers
3 large egg whites
2 tablespoons confectioners' sugar

METHOD

Thaw pastry. Roll thin. Fit into 9½" tart pan. (Or, substitute a prepared pastry shell.) Bake at 350°F until crisp.

In a large bowl, lightly beat eggs, ½ cup sugar, and zest. All sugar need not be dissolved.

In medium saucepan over medium heat, heat juice, ½ cup sugar, and butter until most of the butter has melted. Slowly pour into egg mixture, whisking constantly. Return mixture to saucepan. Over medium heat, cook until shiny, about 5 minutes. Remove from heat before mixture boils. Stir in lavender flowers. Pour into prepared tart shell, cover with plastic wrap, and refrigerate at least 3 hours or overnight.

To serve, preheat broiler. Beat egg whites with remaining 6 tablespoons sugar until stiff peaks form. Spread meringue over cold tart. Brown under broiler. Sprinkle with confectioners' sugar. Refrigerate 30 minutes. Serve cold.

NECTARINES WITH PEPPERS
4 PORTIONS

INGREDIENTS

2 tablespoons minced sweet red pepper
2 tablespoons minced sweet yellow pepper
1½ tablespoons minced fresh cilantro
1 tablespoon minced purple onion
½ teaspoon chili powder
2¼ teaspoons sugar
1 cup water
¼ cup white wine vinegar
4 medium-sized fresh nectarines, peeled,
   halved, and pitted
   fresh cilantro sprigs (optional)

METHOD

In a small bowl, thoroughly combine red and yellow peppers, cilantro, onion, ¼ teaspoon chili powder, and ¼ teaspoon sugar. Let stand at room temperature for 2 hours.

In a small skillet, bring remaining ¼ teaspoon chili powder, remaining 2 teaspoons sugar, water, and vinegar to a boil. Add nectarine halves, spooning liquid over each. Heat through.

Per portion, arrange 2 nectarine halves on plate; fill cavities with pepper mixture. Garnish with cilantro sprig.

Excellent accompaniment for grilled meats and fish.

~ 70 Years of ~
PIONEERING AND PROFESSIONALISM

MEDITERRANEAN SALAD SANDWICH

VICE PRESIDENT,

NORTHEAST REGION

Edward G. Leonard, CMC, AAC

President

Food 1st LLC and

Food 1st Restaurant Corporation

Norwalk, CT

ELECTED NATIONAL OFFICERS 1997-1999

Edward G. Leonard
CMC, AAC

WHO THEY ARE, WHAT THEY DO BEST

A successful consultant, chef, and businessman, Leonard has earned more than 20 gold medals for many types of culinary creations. He also earned three individual gold medals and one team silver medal at the international Culinary Olympics. He is current manager of ACF Culinary Team USA 2000 and has served as vice president of the ACF northeast region since 1997.

Leonard was introduced to the professional culinary scene while serving an apprenticeship under a U. S. Army master chef. He was educated at Eli Whitney's culinary program in Connecticut, The Culinary Institute of America, and on European study tours. In addition, he studied sales and business at Thamside Management School in London, England.

Among many honors accorded this ACF-certified master chef was an invitation to present the commencement address at the CIA in 1994. He is recipient of an ACF President's Medallion, the ACF northeast region's Chef

VEGETABLE PIZZA

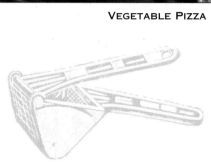

Professionalism Award, Holland's Crystal Chef Award, the business-development award of TrustHouse Forte, and two Chef of the Year awards from the International Chefs Association/ACF Big Apple Chapter.

A frequent speaker and demonstrator, Leonard has made presentations at the New York Hotel/Motel Show, ACF national conventions, and at several resorts. For ComSource, he has appeared in training videos on international cuisine; a recent production featured him and Martin Yan. Leonard has also appeared on television cooking programs, and his work is included in *The Art of Garde Manger* by Fritz Sonnenschmidt, CMC, AAC, the German edition of the 1992 Culinary Olympics book, and in the foodservice press.

Leonard donates many hours at benefits and fund-raisers for Easter seals, American Culinary Federation Chef and Child Foundation, and Norwalk Community College, on whose board he serves.

In his profession, his special abilities include organization, implementation, communication, training versatility, sales, and marketing. He has held his present positions since 1993 and 1996, directing a culinary, marketing, training, and development company, as well as a corporation that operates 14 outlets of an upscale business-dining operation. In the past, he was employed as an executive vice president of sales and marketing, regional vice president of food and beverage operations, director of operations, regional manager, and corporate executive chef.

ROASTED PUMPKIN SOUP
6 TO 8 PORTIONS

INGREDIENTS
- peanut oil as needed
- 1¼ cups unsalted butter
- ½ cup leeks, cut in 1" slices, thoroughly washed, and drained
- 1 cup diced smoked or cured Virginia ham
- 1 tablespoon allspice
- ½ teaspoon cinnamon
- 3 teaspoons brown sugar
- 4 slices raisin bread, cut in 1/4" cubes
- 3- to 5-pound pumpkin, cleaned and seeds removed
- 1 tablespoon walnut oil
- ¼ cup minced shallots
- 1 clove garlic, minced
- ¼ cup diced celery
- 1½ tablespoons flour
- 3 cups chicken stock
- 2 teaspoons maple syrup
- ½ teaspoon ground nutmeg
- ¼ teaspoon white pepper
- salt to taste
- 1 cup heavy cream, reduced

METHOD
In a skillet, heat 1 tablespoon peanut oil until hot. Add 1 tablespoon butter and leeks.

Sauté until leeks begin to caramelize. Add ½ cup ham; sauté 1 to 2 minutes. Reserve.

Thoroughly combine 1 cup butter, allspice, ½ teaspoon cinnamon, and 1 teaspoon brown sugar. Form into cylinder in plastic wrap; then wrap in baking paper. Roll, and tie at ends. Freeze until firm.

Bake bread cubes at 350°F until golden brown and crisp.

Rub pumpkin lightly with peanut oil. Roast in 375°F oven until tender and brown. Cool. Scoop out flesh; discard shell. Purée flesh and reserve 2 to 2½ cups.

In 4-quart saucepan, heat walnut oil and remaining 3 tablespoons butter. Add shallots and garlic; sauté until tender. Add celery and remaining ½ cup ham; sauté 2 to 3 minutes. Blend in flour; cook 2 to 3 minutes.

Remove from heat. Gradually whisk in stock, then pumpkin purée. Return to heat. Simmer 5 to 10 minutes, whisking or stirring often.

Stir in remaining 2 teaspoons brown sugar, maple syrup, remaining ½ teaspoon cinnamon, nutmeg, pepper, salt, and cream. Simmer 5 to 7 minutes longer.

Garnish each warmed individual soup bowl with 1 slice spiced butter, a little of the leek-ham mixture, and a few croutons. Ladle soup into garnished bowls and serve.

TAPENADE
ABOUT 3 CUPS

INGREDIENTS

- 2 cloves fresh garlic
- 4 cloves roasted garlic, puréed
- 1 cup kalamata olives, pits removed
- 1 cup cured Italian olives, pits removed
- 5 fresh anchovy fillets, cleaned
- 1 tablespoon capers, rinsed and drained
- 1 teaspoon chopped fresh sage
- 1 teaspoon chopped fresh basil
- 2 tablespoons fresh lime juice
- 6-8 tablespoons virgin cold-pressed olive oil
  Tuscan toast

METHOD

Put garlic, garlic purée, kalamata olives, Italian olives, anchovies, and capers in food processor. Pulse in sage, basil, and lime juice. With motor running slowly, add 6 tablespoons oil. Process until smooth, adding more oil if needed for flavor and consistency.

Serve on toast, or use as finishing ingredient for sauces to be served with fish and chicken.

TOMATO FONDUE
12 PORTIONS

INGREDIENTS

- 1 loaf Tuscan-style or crusty Italian-style bread, cut in 1" cubes
  extra-virgin olive oil as needed
  black pepper as needed
  grated Parmesan cheese as needed
- 1 small onion, diced
- 5 cloves garlic, sliced
- 3 tablespoons butter
- 3 cups heavy cream
- 15 fully ripe plum tomatoes
- ½ cup tomato paste
  salt as needed
- 1 tablespoon sugar
- ½ cup dry red wine
- 2 tablespoons minced fresh basil

METHOD

Toss bread in some oil, pepper, and cheese. Bake at 350°F until golden brown on all sides. Let rest 1 hour.

Sauté onion and garlic in butter until tender. Add to cream; reduce by ⅓ at low heat. Reserve.

Wash, dry, and core tomatoes; cut each in half. Toss with enough oil to coat. Arrange on baking pan in one layer, skin sides up. Roast at 375 to 400°F until skins begin to brown and lift away from flesh. Remove from oven. Pop off skins. Purée in blender or food processor.

In a skillet, start cooking 2 tablespoons oil and tomato paste. Stir in salt and pepper to taste and sugar. Cook for 6 to 8 minutes. Deglaze pan with wine. Cook 5 to 8 minutes longer. Stir into cream mixture. Add tomato purée, basil, and 3 tablespoons Parmesan. Blend well while simmering; adjust salt and pepper as needed.

Serve in fondue pot, with bread in separate bowl. Provide fondue forks, lobster forks, or toothpicks for spearing bread and dipping in fondue.

MEDITERRANEAN SALAD SANDWICH
8 PORTIONS

INGREDIENTS

- 2 24"-long loaves crusty French bread
  cold-pressed virgin olive oil as needed
  aged red-wine vinegar as needed
- 4 cloves honey-roasted garlic
- 8 plum tomatoes, peeled, seeded, and diced
  kosher salt as needed
  pinch crushed red pepper
- 1 recipe tapenade (see above)
- 2 6-ounce cans solid-packed white tuna, drained
- 4 stalks celery, peeled and diced
- 1 sweet red onion, peeled and sliced paper-thin
- ¾ cup green olives without pits
- ½ cup grated Parmesan cheese
- 4 bunches arugula, washed, drained, and dried
- 8 hard-cooked eggs, sliced

METHOD

Cut each loaf of bread in half lengthwise; scoop out and discard a little of the insides. Arrange each half, cut side up, on broiler pan. Toast.

In a food processor, purée 6 tablespoons oil, 2 tablespoons vinegar, garlic, and 4 diced tomatoes. Season with kosher salt and red pepper. Brush or spoon this dressing evenly on each of the four half-loaves. Spread tapenade evenly on each half.

In a bowl, lightly toss tuna, remaining 4 diced tomatoes, celery, onion, olives, cheese, and 2 tablespoons oil. Season to taste with salt and pepper.

On each of two bottom halves of bread, arrange arugula and sliced eggs. Season with salt and pepper. If desired, drizzle with a little oil and vinegar. Spread tuna mixture on each bottom half. Place each top half of bread on its bottom. Wrap tightly in plastic. Refrigerate for 2 hours. Cut each loaf into 4 sections and enjoy!

GRILLED CHICKEN INSALATA
8 PORTIONS

INGREDIENTS

8 5-ounce boneless, skinless chicken breasts
   extra-virgin olive oil as needed
   salt to taste
   pepper to taste
1 tablespoon sugar
1 tablespoon fresh thyme
1 cup peeled, diced, salted eggplant
1 cup diced red bell pepper
¼ cup pitless cured black olives
8 Roma tomatoes
2 quarts chopped romaine
8 ounces shaved table ricotta
1 tablespoon balsamic vinegar
10 ounces baby penne pasta
2 cups roasted-garlic vinaigrette

METHOD

Marinate chicken in mixture of enough oil to coat breasts well plus salt, pepper, sugar, and thyme. Cover and refrigerate 30 minutes.

Char-grill chicken until cooked and tender. Slice each breast on bias; reserve.

In a hot skillet in a little oil, sear eggplant. Add peppers and olives during last 1 minute of cooking. Set aside.

Blanch tomatoes; peel and cut in quarters. Remove seeds and reserve.

Combine romaine, ricotta, and eggplant mixture. Toss with 2 tablespoons oil and vinegar. Cook pasta al dente; drain well. While hot, add to romaine-ricotta-vegetable mixture with enough vinaigrette to moisten. Toss well.

Serve insalata in individual bowls, each portion topped with chicken. Serve remaining vinaigrette on the side.

VEAL SHANKS BRACIOLA STYLE
12 PORTIONS

INGREDIENTS

2 shanks of milk-fed veal, each 2½ to 3
   pounds
4 cloves garlic, minced
3 tablespoons chopped fresh parsley
¼ cup grated Pecorino Romano cheese
½ tablespoon grated lemon rind
   kosher salt as needed
   black pepper as needed
   olive oil as needed
1 onion, diced
3 cloves garlic, sliced
2 carrots, diced
3 tablespoons tomato paste
1 cup dry red wine
2 cups crushed fresh Roma tomatoes
3 cups tomato sauce

METHOD

Remove bones from shanks, keeping meat from each in one piece. Leave marrow bones whole, or cut into 2" pieces; reserve.

With a mallet, flatten meat. Mix minced garlic, parsley, cheese, and rind. Season shanks with salt and pepper to taste. Fill cavities with garlic-parsley-cheese mixture; roll each and tie with twine.

In oil in a brazier, brown meat well on all sides. Remove from pot and reserve.

Add a little more oil to brazier, and sauté onion, sliced garlic, and carrots. When lightly brown, add tomato paste. Cook and stir well. Deglaze pan with wine.

Add crushed tomatoes and tomato sauce; stir. Add bones. Place shanks on top and cover. Braise in 350°F oven until tender. Remove shanks and bones.

Season sauce to taste and adjust consistency if needed.

Slice and serve shanks; or, for color, roast first in hot (450°F) oven. Serve with marrow, sauce, soft polenta, and sautéed escarole.

VEGETABLE PIZZA
2 PIZZAS/10 PORTIONS

INGREDIENTS
- 1 teaspoon sugar
- 2 teaspoons dry yeast
- ¼ teaspoon salt
- 2 cups warm (about 80°F) water
- 11 tablespoons virgin olive oil
- 1½ cups oat flour
- 1½ cups whole-wheat flour
- 1½ cups bread flour
- 1 finely diced onion
- 1 finely diced bell pepper
- 1 finely diced small zucchini
- 1 tablespoon finely chopped garlic
- 2 tablespoons chopped fresh oregano
- 2 tablespoons chopped fresh parsley
- 3 tablespoons chopped fresh basil
- 2 teaspoons coarsely ground black pepper
- 1 quart peeled, seeded, chopped tomatoes
- 1 thinly sliced zucchini
- 4 ounces fresh mushrooms, thinly sliced
- 1 cup fresh tomatoes, peeled, seeded, and diced
- 12 ounces coarsely grated mozzarella cheese

METHOD
Add sugar, yeast, and salt to warm water; mix thoroughly. Allow to stand for a few minutes until foam begins to form on top. Add 6 tablespoons oil, oat flour, and whole-wheat flour; mix until smooth. If using a bread machine or electric mixer, mix at high speed for only a few seconds.

Add bread flour, a little at a time, until correct consistency is achieved. (Dough should roll freely on a lightly floured surface without sticking to the fingers.) Cover dough with plastic wrap; refrigerate at least 2 hours.

For sauce, sauté onions, peppers, diced zucchini, and garlic in 4 tablespoons oil. Add oregano, parsley, 2 tablespoons basil basil, black pepper, and 1 quart tomatoes. Simmer for 1 hour.

For topping, sauté zucchini, mushrooms, and 1 cup tomatoes in remaining 1 tablespoon oil until tender but not brown.

Divide dough into 2 equal portions. Roll out each to thickness of ¼". Place on shallow pans (shape unimportant). Cover generously with sauce, spreading evenly. Cover both pizzas with cheese; distribute topping over cheese. Sprinkle pies with remaining 1 tablespoon basil.

Bake at 500°F for 20 minutes, until crusts are well-browned.

SAUCE TAPENADE
ABOUT 1½ CUPS

INGREDIENTS
- 1½ cups dry white wine
- 3 diced shallots
  about ¼ cup heavy cream
- 1 tablespoon sour cream
- 6 to 8 tablespoons unsalted butter, diced
- ¾ cup tapenade (see recipe page 55)

METHOD
In saucepan, simmer wine and shallots until reduced to ⅓ cup. Strain, discarding shallots. Return liquid to saucepan. Whisk in heavy cream and sour cream; place on low heat. Gradually add butter, whisking well until butter is just melted. Whisk in tapenade. If needed, add a little more cream. Serve over fish or chicken.

STRAWBERRIES WITH BALSAMIC SYRUP AND POUND-CAKE CROUTONS
8 PORTIONS

INGREDIENTS
- 2 cups aged balsamic vinegar
- 1 quart fresh ripe strawberries, hulled and halved
- 2 tablespoons brown sugar
- 3 tablespoons orange juice
- 1 cup diced pound cake
- 2 tablespoons melted unsalted butter
- 1 cup heavy cream
  granulated sugar to taste
- ½ tablespoon vanilla extract
  ground chocolate as needed

METHOD
In saucepan, bring vinegar to a boil; reduce to a little less than 1 cup. Cool.

Toss berries with brown sugar and juice; let stand 1 hour.

Toss cake with butter; toast in hot (450°F) oven until cubes resemble croutons.

Whip cream with sugar and vanilla until medium-firm peaks form.

In each of 8 wine glasses, place an equal amount of half the pound-cake croutons. Fill with berries. Drizzle balsamic syrup over berries. Top with remaining croutons and dollop of cream. Garnish with a sprinkling of ground chocolate.

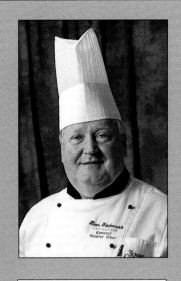

VICE PRESIDENT,

SOUTHEAST REGION

Klaus D. Friedenreich, CMC, AAC

Director of Culinary Arts

The Art Institute of Fort Lauderdale

Fort Lauderdale, FL

SEARED LOIN OF VENISON WITH SPAETZLE

ELECTED NATIONAL OFFICERS 1997-1999

Klaus D. Friedenreich
CMC, AAC

WHO THEY ARE, WHAT THEY DO BEST

*I*n 1964, Friedenreich emigrated from Germany where he had served a culinary apprenticeship and studied general food administration. For the next 16 years, he was employed by American restaurants and hotels. After seven years in the northeast, he accepted a position as one of the inaugural chefs at Walt Disney World in 1971. He later was executive chef of Carlton House and Maison et Jardin.

1980 was a banner year for Friedenreich. He served as captain of the U.S. culinary team that earned 30 gold medals and won first place in hot food (and, thus, the world championship for the United States for the first time) at the international Culinary Olympics in Frankfurt, Germany. He also was awarded an individual gold medal. And, he opened Klaus' Cuisine of Daytona Beach. During the six years he owned and successfully operated his own fine-dining restaurant, it was awarded five Golden Spoon Awards and named one of the top 50 restaurants in Florida.

After several executive chefs' positions, during which he cooked for more than one U.S. president, he joined the U.S. Chefs Open as executive vice president in 1986.

Currently a member of ACF Greater Fort Lauderdale Chapter, Friedenreich is a founder and past president of ACF Central Florida Chapter. A certified ACF culinary show judge since 1974, he is past chair of ACF's national culinary committee. He also has served as ACF national secretary-treasurer.

Friedenreich has earned numerous accolades including ACF Culinarian of the Year Award in 1984, the Antonin Carême Medal in 1985, and a silver medal in the first ACF national nutritional competition in 1992. He has been elected to membership in the Honorary Order of the Golden Toque and Confrerie de la Chaines des Rotisseurs. He is a founder and past president of the Central Florida Chapter of Les Toques Blanches. Among his many awards are first prizes in ice-carving, grand prize and best of show in culinary salons, and many gold medals in a variety of professional culinary competitions.

In 1993, Friedenreich earned designation as an ACF-certified master chef. For the last six years, he has directed his career to culinary education. At The Art Institute of Fort Lauderdale, he has built a department of nine instructors and developed 18-month degree and 12-month diploma programs for the school's 200 full- and part-time culinary students.

HONEY-MUSTARD GLAZED SALMON

POTATO-LEEK SOUP (KARTOFFELCREMESUPPE)
4 PORTIONS

INGREDIENTS
2 tablespoons unsalted butter or margarine
2 large yellow onions, peeled and thinly sliced
1 small leek, trimmed, thoroughly washed, and thinly sliced
1 small stalk celery, thinly sliced
2 thick slices double-smoked bacon, halved crosswise
1 teaspoon dried marjoram, crumbled
1 teaspoon dried thyme, crumbled
¼ teaspoon freshly grated nutmeg
1 pound Maine or other eastern potatoes, peeled and thinly sliced
1 quart rich chicken stock, preferably homemade
1 teaspoon salt
¼ teaspoon freshly ground black pepper
2 tablespoons minced fresh chives

METHOD
In a large heavy saucepan over moderate heat, melt butter. Add onions, leek, celery, bacon, marjoram, thyme, and nutmeg. Stir-fry about 2 minutes until glazed. Reduce heat to low, cover, and steam 15 minutes until onions are very limp. Remove and discard bacon.

Increase heat to medium. Add potatoes and stock. Bring to simmer, uncovered, and adjust heat so stock bubbles gently. Cover and simmer 40 minutes, until potatoes are mushy. Remove from heat. Cool soup, still covered, 15 minutes.

In batches, purée soup at high speed in food processor or blender for 1 minute. Return to pan. Stir in salt and pepper. Taste and adjust seasonings. Heat, uncovered, to serving temperature. Ladle into bowls and garnish each portion with chives.

TENDER GREENS WITH CITRUS VINAIGRETTE
4 PORTIONS

INGREDIENTS
- ½ cup light olive oil
- 1 tablespoon tarragon vinegar
- 2 tablespoons lemon and/or lime juice
- 1 tablespoon shallots, finely diced
- salt as needed
- freshly ground black pepper as needed
- 8 ounces tender greens such as mâche (also called corn salad, field salad, field lettuce, and lamb's lettuce) or tat-soi
- ¼ cup cucumber, peeled, seeded, and diced
- ¼ tomato, peeled, seeded, and diced
- 4 slices Melba toast

METHOD

Thoroughly whisk oil, vinegar, juice, shallots, salt, and pepper.

Wash, drain, and dry greens; toss with vinaigrette. Arrange on four salad plates. Garnish each with cucumbers, tomato concassé, and a slice of toast.

HONEY-MUSTARD GLAZED SALMON
12 PORTIONS

INGREDIENTS
- ½ cup Dijon mustard
- 1 tablespoon light soy sauce
- ¼ cup honey
- ¼ teaspoon cracked caraway seeds
- 1 tablespoon cracked mustard seeds
- juice and zest of 1 lemon
- 2 shallots, chopped
- ¼ cup light olive oil
- 12 4-ounce salmon fillets, all bones and skin removed

Sauce:
- 2 tablespoons minced shallots
- ¼ cup butter
- 1 cup dry white wine
- 2 cups orange juice
- juice of 2 lemons
- ½ cup Dijon mustard
- ¼ cup honey

Garnish:
- 12 orange sections
- zest of 2 oranges, blanched

METHOD

Thoroughly combine first eight ingredients. Coat each fillet with marinade; cover and refrigerate for 1 hour.

In a very hot heavy skillet, sear fillets, two or three at a time, on both sides, until slightly browned. Transfer to a baking sheet. Bake at 350°F for 5 to 7 minutes, basting 3 or 4 times with remaining marinade.

For sauce, sweat shallots in butter. Deglaze pan with white wine; reduce liquid to syrup consistency. Add orange and lemon juices; reduce to half. Whisk in mustard and honey to form an emulsion.

Serve salmon and sauce with Dijon mashed potatoes (recipe on page 61) and braised mustard greens (recipe below). Arrange each plate as follows: pipe potatoes in center; top with a round of greens; center a salmon fillet on greens; surround with sauce; and garnish with an orange section and orange zest.

BRAISED MUSTARD GREENS
12 PORTIONS

INGREDIENTS
- 2 pounds mustard greens
- salt as needed
- boiling water as needed
- ½ cup diced bacon
- ¼ cup butter
- ½ cup diced onions
- ½ cup diced celeriac
- ½ cup diced carrots
- 2 bay leaves
- 2 sprigs thyme
- 2 cups well-seasoned chicken stock

METHOD

Blanch greens in salted boiling water; drain, refresh with cold water, and dry.

Render bacon fat; discard most of the drippings. Add butter and onions; sweat. Add celeriac and carrots; sweat. Stir in bay leaves and thyme. Spread onion mixture in bottom of a small roasting pan; spread greens evenly on top. Add stock; cover pan. Bake at 350°F for 10 to 15 minutes. Remove from oven; mix well. Keep warm or serve at once.

⁓ 70 Years of ⁓
PIONEERING AND PROFESSIONALISM

SEARED LOIN OF VENISON WITH SAUCE POIVRADE
6 PORTIONS

INGREDIENTS

- 5 pound saddle of venison
  cooking oil as needed
- 1 cup chopped carrots
- 1 cup chopped onions
- 1¼ cups vinegar
- ⅞ cup dry white wine
  pinch thyme
- ½ bay leaf, crushed
  few parsley stalks
  water as needed
  salt as needed
  pepper as needed
- 4 ounces ground venison leg meat
- 4 ounces ground pork
- 2 ounces pork fat
- 2 egg whites
- ¼-⅓ cup cream
- 1 pound assorted mushrooms,
  cleaned and sliced
- 8 ounces pork caul
- 12 crushed peppercorns
- 5 tablespoons butter

METHOD

Cut out loin (weighing about 2 pounds) and remove silver skin. Wrap and refrigerate loin until ready to use.

To make brown stock, brown venison bones and trimmings well. In a large pot in ½ cup oil, cook carrots and onions until well-colored. Drain off and discard drippings. Moisten with vinegar and wine; reduce completely. Add thyme, bay leaf, parsley, and water to cover ingredients well. Add bones and trimmings. Cover and cook in 300°F oven for 3½ to 4 hours.

Season loin with salt and pepper. Sear in a little hot oil, keeping meat rare. Cool.

Process ground venison, ground pork, pork fat, and egg whites in food processor until smooth. Season with salt and pepper. Add enough cream to produce a smooth consistency.

Briefly blanch or steam mushrooms; drain and dry.

Place forcemeat on a sheet of plastic wrap; with a spatula, spread it to about 12" x 12". Sprinkle mushrooms over forcemeat; then press them into the forcemeat.

Set seared loin at one end of forcemeat; wrap forcemeat around loin. Spread caul out; wrap it around loin. Refrigerate at least 30 minutes. Roast at 375°F for 45 to 60 minutes.

To finish sauce poivrade, strain venison stock; you should have about 9 cups. Eight minutes before serving, stir in peppercorns; boil uncovered until reduced to 4½ cups. Stir in butter; add salt and pepper to taste. Keep warm.

Serve venison with sauce poivrade, spaetzle (recipe below), and haricots vert.

SPAETZLE (TINY GERMAN NOODLES)
6 PORTIONS

INGREDIENTS

- 1 cup sifted all-purpose flour
- ⅛ teaspoon freshly grated nutmeg
  salt as needed
- 3 large eggs
- 6 tablespoons milk
  water as needed
- 3 tablespoons melted unsalted
  butter or margarine

METHOD

In a small bowl, combine flour, nutmeg, and ¼ teaspoon salt. Make a well in the center.

Whisk eggs with milk. Pour into well of dry ingredients. Beat hard with a wooden spoon until batter is bubbly and elastic. Or, mix in a food processor; then give batter 3 or 4 one-minute pulses until smooth and elastic.

Push batter through a spaetzle-maker or colander into a large kettle of rapidly boiling salted water. Cook uncovered for 8 minutes, stirring occasionally.

With a slotted spoon lift spaetzle to a large bowl of ice water. Let stand until ready to serve, but no longer than 2 hours.

Drain spaetzle in a colander; then warm 4 to 5 minutes in melted butter in a large skillet over medium–low heat, stirring occasionally. Serve at once.

DIJON MASHED POTATOES
12 PORTIONS

INGREDIENTS

- 3 pounds potatoes, peeled and cut into
  small pieces
- ½ cup butter
- ¼ cup Dijon mustard
- ½ cup light cream
- ¼ teaspoon nutmeg
- ¼ teaspoon white pepper
- ½ teaspoon kosher salt

METHOD

Steam potatoes in top of double-boiler over simmering water, or in a steamer. When tender, drain well and mash with a potato masher in cooking pot. Stir in butter. Stir in mustard and cream. Season with nutmeg, pepper, and salt. Keep warm or serve at once.

PORK LOIN WITH MOREL STUFFING
6 PORTIONS

INGREDIENTS

1½ ounces small dried morels
 2 cups boiling water
 3 tablespoons extra-virgin olive oil
½ cup chopped shallots
 1 clove garlic, minced
¾ cup fine fresh bread crumbs
¼ cup chopped fresh parsley leaves, washed
    and dried before chopping
    salt and pepper as needed
    3- to 3½-pound center-cut boneless
    pork loin, about 3½" thick
 2 tablespoons fresh lime juice
 2 cups rich veal stock or demi-glace

METHOD

In a small bowl, soak morels in boiling water for 30 minutes. With a slotted spoon, transfer to paper towels to drain.

Pour soaking liquid through a sieve lined with a dampened coffee filter or paper towel into a small saucepan. Simmer until reduced to ⅓ cup, about 10 minutes. Add ⅓ of the morels and reserve. Finely chop remaining morels. (Morels may be prepared to this point one day ahead, covered, and refrigerated.)

In a large skillet, heat 1½ tablespoons oil over medium-high heat until hot but not smoking. Sauté shallots and garlic until softened. Transfer to a bowl. Stir in chopped morels, crumbs, parsley, and salt and pepper to taste. (This stuffing may be made one day ahead, covered, and refrigerated. Bring to room temperature before proceeding.)

With paper towels, pat loin dry. Beginning in center of one end, with a long, thin, sharp knife, make a lengthwise incision toward the center of the loin. Repeat the procedure at the center of the other end, to complete an incision running through the center of the pork. With the handle of a wooden spoon (or your fingers), open the incision to create a 1½"-wide opening.

Working from both ends of the loin, pack stuffing into opening, pushing toward the center. Season outside of meat with salt and pepper.

In a skillet, heat remaining 1½ tablespoons oil over high heat until just smoking. Brown loin on all sides, about 1½ minutes total. Transfer pork to a roasting pan. Roast at 375°F in center of oven about 1 hour, or until a meat thermometer inserted in center of meat (to one side of the stuffing) registers 160°F. Transfer pork to a cutting board; let stand 10 minutes.

Add lime juice to roasting pan and deglaze over medium heat, scraping up browned bits. Add stock or demi-glace and reserved morel liquid with morels. Simmer, stirring occasionally, 5 minutes.

Slice loin and serve with sauce.

GINGERBREAD BAVARIAN WITH RAISIN SAUCE
10 PORTIONS

INGREDIENTS

 1 quart milk
 1 vanilla bean, split
 1 cup sugar
 8 egg yolks
 1 ounce unflavored powdered gelatin
 2 tablespoons kirsch
 2 tablespoons brandy
¼ cup water
 1 cup heavy cream, whipped until stiff but
    not dry
 6 egg whites, whipped until soft peaks form
 1 cup gingerbread cookies, finely chopped

Sauce:
 1 cup apple cider or apple juice
 3 tablespoons brown sugar
 2 tablespoons apple brandy
¼ teaspoon ground cinnamon
    few grains ground nutmeg
½ vanilla bean
 1 teaspoon (or more, or less) arrowroot
 1 ounce golden raisins (or currants)

METHOD

In top of double-boiler, bring milk, vanilla bean, and ½ cup sugar to a boil. Remove vanilla bean. In a bowl, beat yolks with remaining ½ cup sugar; temper gradually with a little of the hot vanilla-flavored milk. Pour egg mixture into top of double–boiler with remaining milk and mix. Cook over simmering water to 180°F. Strain and cool.

In top of a clean double-boiler, soften gelatin in mixture of kirsch, brandy, and water. Heat over simmering water until clear. Mix into vanilla sauce. Fold in whipped cream. Fold in beaten egg whites. Fold in cookie crumbs. Turn into bowl. Cover and refrigerate for several hours.

For sauce, combine all ingredients except arrowroot and raisins. Bring to boil; lower heat and simmer 1 minute. Thicken to desired consistency with arrowroot. Stir in raisins. Cool. Cover and refrigerate until serving time.

To serve, spoon Bavarian into stemmed glasses and top with sauce.

≈ 70 Years of ≈
PIONEERING AND PROFESSIONALISM

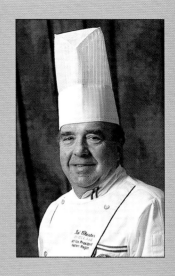

FRUITS DE MER WITH SAFFRON SAUCE

VICE PRESIDENT,

WESTERN REGION

Bob Chester, CEC, CCE, AAC

Owner/Operator

Creative Ice Sculptures, It's All About

Profit, and Chef's Signature Products

San Diego, CA

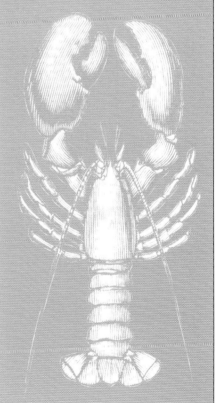

ELECTED NATIONAL OFFICERS 1997-1999

Bob Chester
CEC, CCE, AAC

WHO THEY ARE, WHAT THEY DO BEST

*A*s a teenager, Chester launched his culinary career at Oakland Hills Country Club in Birmingham, MI, followed by positions at the Detroit Yacht Club and the Sheraton Cadillac Hotel, Detroit, as executive sous chef. Sheraton then transferred him to Kentucky, where he became the corporation's youngest ever executive chef at the Sheraton Louisville. After being named executive chef of the Sheraton Chicago Hotel, he joined ACF Chicago Chefs of Cuisine, Inc.

Following positions with Holiday Inns as food and beverage director, Sheraton lured him to its new Sheraton Harbor Island Hotel in San Diego, and he transferred his membership to ACF Chefs de Cuisine Association of San Diego. He was subsequently offered positions as executive assistant general manager of food and beverage at the Sheraton Four Ambassadors, Miami; as food and beverage manager at Vacation Village Resort, San Diego; and as cor-

**VEAL CHOPS
WITH RED PEPPER SAUCE**

porate executive chef of Hamilton Meat Co., San Diego. Chester now owns and operates three companies, which provide a variety of culinary-related services including consulting and brokerage functions.

After earning his California teaching credentials at San Diego State College, Chester served as a culinary instructor at Mesa College, San Diego, for 17 years. As ACF vice president of the western region for the past two years, Chester has spearheaded and/or been involved in a number of achievements by ACF chapters in his area. Among them: ACF region of the year; increases of 1,100 percent in Are You Really ACF award applications, 800 percent in regional Chef of the Year applications, and 500 percent in regional Chef Professionalism applications; inauguration of a western regional newsletter to chapter presidents and area coordinators; five new chapters chartered in 1999; six new chapters being developed; one chapter being reactivated; and initiation of lifetime membership status for ACF senior chefs.

Under Chester's leadership, for the first time in ACF history, the western region includes a chapter located on a U.S. Marine Corps base in Okinawa, Japan. He also was instrumental in arranging the first-ever American Academy of Chefs dinner at a regional conference, held in 1999 in Las Vegas. In addition, that conference hosted 700 attendees, including 16 student culinary teams, and presented the regional finals of the Baron H. Galand Culinary Knowledge Bowl as part of its general session. Other accomplishments of the region during Chester's vice presidency include plans for the selection of a western ACF junior member of the year, to be announced annually at regional conferences beginning in 2000.

PETITE FILETS MIGNON ROSSINI WITH MADEIRA SAUCE
4 PORTIONS

INGREDIENTS
- 4 ¼" slices baguette
- 5 tablespoons butter or margarine
- 2 tablespoons peeled, chopped shallots
- ½ cup brown stock
- ½ cup Madeira
- 1 cup demi-glace
   salt as needed
   black pepper as needed
- 4 6-ounce tenderloin steaks
- 2 tablespoons vegetable oil
- 4 2-ounce slices raw duck liver

METHOD
Spread baguette slices with 2 tablespoons butter. Arrange on nonstick baking sheet. Bake at 350°F about 6 minutes until well-browned. Remove from oven; set aside.

In a small saucepan, melt 1 tablespoon butter. Add shallots; sauté 1 minute. Add stock and wine; cook until mixture is reduced by ½. Add demi-glace; continue cooking and stirring for 10 minutes. Strain through a fine sieve into a small saucepan; blend in remaining 2 tablespoons butter. Season with salt and pepper. Keep warm

Season steaks with salt and pepper. In a heavy skillet, heat oil; sear steaks for 2 minutes on each side. Transfer to baking sheet; place in 400°F oven. Bake about 10 minutes (medium-rare).

In same skillet, sauté liver for 15 seconds on each side.

On each warm dinner plate, place a steak off-center. Place a crouton with liver on it to left of steak. Spoon on sauce, covering half the steak's surface. Divide and arrange vegetables (tourné potatoes, baby carrots, baby zucchini, and haricots verts are suggested) around steak presentation.

AMARETTO PEA PODS
6 PORTIONS

INGREDIENTS

- water as needed
- 1 teaspoon salt
- 12 ounces fresh pea pods, washed, drained, and trimmed
- 3 tablespoons unsalted butter
- 1½ tablespoons amaretto
- 1½ teaspoons fresh lime juice
- 1 egg yolk, slightly beaten

METHOD

Fill a large skillet ⅔-full of water; bring to boil and add salt. Drop pea pods in boiling water. Cover, return to boil, and cook for 2 minutes. Pea pods will be slightly crunchy. Remove from heat, drain, cover, and keep warm.

In a small saucepan, melt butter over low heat until it is golden. Pour into a small bowl. Cool slightly. With a fork, whisk in amaretto until smooth. Whisk in lime juice. Add a small amount of butter mixture to egg yolk; whisk again. Add remaining amaretto butter to yolk and whisk until smooth. Pour over pea pods and serve.

Note: If amaretto butter separates, warm it slightly and whisk again.

NETTED FRUITS DE MER WITH SAFFRON SAUCE
4 PORTIONS

INGREDIENTS

- 2 quarts water
- salt as needed
- 3 tablespoons vegetable oil
- 8 ounces black linguini
- ½ cup fish stock
- ¼ cup dry white wine
- ⅛ teaspoon + ½ teaspoon saffron strands
- ½ cup heavy cream
- 3 tablespoons butter or margarine, softened
- 1 clove garlic, peeled and finely minced
- white pepper as needed
- 8 ounce lobster tail (including shell), cut into 4 pieces
- 4 large scallops
- 8 large (16-20 count) shrimp, shelled and deveined
- 4 Dungeness crab claws, cooked and drained

METHOD

In a large saucepan, bring water to boil. Add 1 teaspoon salt, vegetable oil, and linguini. Cook 7 minutes. Drain; set aside and keep warm.

In a small saucepan, combine stock, wine, and ⅛ teaspoon saffron strands. Stir and simmer until mixture is reduced by half. Add cream; cook until slightly thickened. Keep warm.

In a small mixing bowl, thoroughly combine butter, garlic, and salt and white pepper to taste. Arrange lobster tail, scallops, and shrimp on a greased baking pan; brush with garlic butter. Bake at 400°F about 8 minutes. Remove from oven. Add crab claws. Top scallops only with remaining ½ teaspoon saffron. Bake 5 minutes longer. Remove from oven; keep warm.

Spoon saffron sauce onto each of four fish plates. Lay strands of linguini horizontally and vertically over sauce to create net effect. Arrange seafood on linguini net.

CHICKEN SALTIMBOCCA WITH MARSALA SAUCE
4 PORTIONS

INGREDIENTS

- 4 6-ounce whole boneless chicken breasts
- 4 thin slices prosciutto, about 2" wide x 4" long
- 4 thin slices fontina or Bel Paese cheese
- 8 fresh sage leaves or 1 teaspoon crumbled dried sage
- 1 cup + 2 tablespoons chicken stock
- 1½ cups Marsala
- ½ cup butter or margarine cut in small pieces
- 1 tablespoon cornstarch dissolved in 1 tablespoon cold water
- ½ teaspoon salt
- ⅛ teaspoon white pepper
- ½ bunch fresh basil leaves

METHOD

Lay chicken breasts skin sides down. Flatten by hitting with a mallet. Cover each with slice each of prosciutto and cheese. Sprinkle sage over cheese. Roll up chicken and arrange on greased baking pan, seams sides down. Add 2 tablespoons stock. Bake at 375°F for 25 to 30 minutes until thoroughly cooked. Remove from oven to warm platter; keep warm.

Pour drippings into small saucepan. Add remaining 1 cup stock and wine. Cook and stir over medium heat until mixture is reduced by half. Lower heat; whisk in butter or margarine one piece at a time. Add cornstarch mixture, salt, and pepper. Strain into top of double-boiler. Keep warm over simmering water.

To serve, cut each breast into 5 slices. Fan slices down right-hand side of dinner plate. Spoon about ¼ cup sauce over chicken. As accompaniments, arrange braised endive on lower left-hand side of plate, risotto on upper left-hand side. Garnish center of plate with basil.

VEAL CHOPS WITH RED PEPPER SAUCE
4 PORTIONS

INGREDIENTS

4   red bell peppers, washed and dried
4   7-ounce, ¾"-thick veal chops cut
      from rack with chine bone removed
      and rib bone intact
     salt as needed
     white pepper as needed
3   tablespoons olive oil
2   tablespoons butter or margarine
1   large red onion, chopped
2   cloves garlic, peeled and coarsely chopped
2   cups dry red wine
⅛   teaspoon cayenne pepper
     black pepper as needed

METHOD

Arrange peppers on nonstick baking sheet; bake at 350°F for 1 hour. Remove from oven and cool. Carefully remove skins, cut into halves, remove seeds, and chop coarsely. Set aside.

Season chops with ½ teaspoon each salt and white pepper. In large skillet, heat oil. Add chops and sear 3 minutes on each side. Remove from skillet; transfer to greased baking pan, and bake in 275°F oven for 10 minutes or until chops have reached desired degree of doneness.

In medium-sized saucepan over medium heat, melt butter or margarine. Add onion, garlic, and peppers. Sauté 3 minutes. Add wine; bring to simmer and cook 8 minutes. Remove from heat. Stir in cayenne and salt and black pepper to taste. Transfer to blender and purée. Remove from blender container to top of double-boiler; keep warm over simmering water.

Spoon red pepper sauce onto lower portion of each of 4 dinner plates. Lay a chop on top of sauce, horizontal to diner. At upper-left, place a mold of polenta with Gorgonzola cheese (see recipe below). At upper-right, arrange spinach (see recipe below).

POLENTA WITH GORGONZOLA CHEESE
4 PORTIONS

INGREDIENTS

2   cups water
½   teaspoon salt
¾   cup coarsely ground cornmeal
¼   teaspoon white pepper
4   ounces Gorgonzola cheese

METHOD

In a heavy saucepan, bring water and salt to a boil. Gradually add cornmeal, a little at a time, whisking constantly. When all the cornmeal has been added, reduce heat and cook 15 minutes, stirring often. Mixture will become very thick. Remove from heat; stir in pepper.

Using a rubber spatula, fill four greased ½-cup timbales with polenta. Pack down firmly with back of spatula. Invert timbales on a cookie sheet. Tap lightly to release polenta. Place 1 ounce of cheese on top of each mold. Bake at 350°F about 2 minutes, until cheese is melted. Use a spatula to transfer polenta to warm dinner plates.

SPINACH WITH PINE NUTS
4 PORTIONS

INGREDIENTS

⅛   cup pine nuts
     salt as needed
4   teaspoons butter or margarine
2   bunches fresh spinach leaves, washed,
      dried, and stems removed
     white pepper as needed

METHOD

Spread pine nuts on nonstick baking sheet. Sprinkle lightly with salt. Bake at 350°F for 3 minutes or until toasted. Remove from oven and set aside.

In a large skillet or wok, melt butter or margarine. Add spinach. Cook, stirring constantly, until wilted. Season with salt and pepper. Gently fold in pine nuts. Remove from heat and serve.

Squash–Blossom Crêpes with Melted Gruyère Cheese and Cream
6 to 8 portions

Ingredients

- 4 poblano chiles, roasted, peeled, seeded, and deveined
- 1 cup cider vinegar
- 1 cup water
- 3 ears of corn, husked
- ⅓ cup olive oil
- 1⅓ cups butter
- 1 onion, finely chopped
- 4 cloves garlic, peeled and finely chopped
- 3 tomatoes, peeled and chopped
- 2¼ pounds squash blossoms (thick outer leaves removed), washed, dried, and chopped
- salt as needed
- pepper as needed
- 10 eggs
- 2 cups flour
- 1 quart milk
- 1¾ cups half-and-half
- 1¼ cups sour cream or crème fraîche
- 5 ounces grated Parmesan cheese
- 14 ounces grated Gruyère or Swiss cheese

Method

In small container, marinate chiles in vinegar and water for 2 hours. Remove chiles; slice into strips, and set aside.

Remove corn kernels from cobs. Blanch kernels in boiling salted water for 8 minutes. Drain; set aside.

In a saucepan, heat oil and ⅓ cup butter. Add onion and garlic; sauté until soft. Add corn, chiles, tomatoes, squash blossoms, salt to taste, and ¼ tablespoon pepper. Simmer 40 minutes or until mixture thickens.

Blend eggs, 1 teaspoon salt, flour, milk, and ½ cup butter.

Over low heat, heat a small skillet; grease lightly with some of remaining butter. Add small amount of batter, tilting pan to create a thin crêpe. Cook until edges begin to dry. Turn over carefully with spatula or fingers. Cook until light brown. Remove from pan. Repeat, using all batter and stacking crêpes on a plate.

Add half-and-half to sour cream or crème fraîche. Add salt and pepper to taste. Set aside.

Lightly mix cheeses. Set aside.

Spoon approximately 2 tablespoons filling onto each crêpe, fold in sides, and loosely roll up. Place seam side down on buttered baking dish.

Cover rolled crêpes with cream mixture; sprinkle with cheese. Bake at 350°F for 40 minutes or until cheese is golden brown. If crusty top is desired, place under broiler briefly.

Serve hot, directly from oven, on warm plates. Accompany with green salad. A great main course at lunch.

Almond Wild Rice
6 portions

Ingredients

- 2 tablespoons vegetable oil
- ½ cup slivered blanched almonds
- 1 medium onion, finely chopped
- 1 tablespoon finely chopped shallots
- 2 tablespoons finely chopped green bell pepper
- 1 clove garlic, peeled and finely chopped
- 1 cup raw wild rice, rinsed three times in cold water and thoroughly drained
- ⅛ teaspoon freshly ground black pepper
- ¼ teaspoon ground cinnamon
- ¼ teaspoon ground nutmeg
- ⅛ teaspoon cumin
- 2½ cups chicken stock, heated

Method

In a skillet, heat oil. Add almonds; stir and cook until slivers are lightly browned. Strain almonds over a saucepan, retaining oil and setting nuts aside.

In saucepan with almond oil, cook and stir onions, shallots, green pepper, and garlic until tender but not brown. Add wild rice, pepper, cinnamon, nutmeg, and cumin. Cook and stir about 5 minutes. Stir in chicken stock.

Place in a casserole and cover. Bake in center of 325°F oven about 1 hour until rice is tender and liquid has been absorbed. Stir rice after it has baked for 30 minutes.

Programs

ACF FORMULA FOR SUCCESS

A **CMC** or **CMPC**, certified master chef or certified master pastry chef, demonstrates the highest degree of knowledge and skills in the culinary profession. He or she serves as a role model not only to students and apprentices, but also to all chefs—certified and not certified—who aspire to achieve master-chef designation. Certification as an executive chef is a prerequisite. The master chef examination stretches over a period of ten days, during which candidates must reside at or near the testing site in order to undergo both written and practical testing in such disciplines as food science, menu development, foodservice management, dining room service and supervision, table-side cooking, cost control, beverage management, baking/pastry/patisserie, charcuterie, cold-buffet preparation, nutritional and dietary cooking, and international, classical, and American cuisines. The day-long, two-part final examination requires preparation of a menu from a lottery of international or classical cuisines and the creation of a multi-course meal from an array of mystery-basket ingredients.

A **CEC**, certified executive chef, is a full-time chef who is responsible for all the culinary units in a restaurant, hotel, club, hospital, or other foodservice establishment, or who is the owner of a foodservice operation. As head of a department or owner of a business, he or she supervises a minimum of five full-time employees who are engaged in food production. He or she is also responsible to top management, who coordinates the CEC's

EDUCATION + CERTIFICATION = OPPORTUNITY + ACHIEVEMENT

Certification within a profession has been defined by the U.S. National Certification Commisson as "career recognition through the evaluation and the approval of individuals engaged in a specific occupation or profession."

ACF is the certification agency for professional culinarians in the United States. Annually, 700 or more applications for certification are reviewed at ACF national headquarters. The average envelope contains 10 pages of forms, certificates, citations, transcripts, and other documentation. The total pages ACF reviews exceeds 12,000 per year, almost 50 pages every work-day.

In addition, ACF verifies all employment and education claims, which may require up to eight telephone calls per applicant. Even so, from start to finish, the process requires only about one month per applicant.

ACF offers members 10 types of professional certification, each of which must be earned through culinary education, professional experience, testing, and documentation. Before submitting to an examination, every candidate for certification must have earned a minimum number of points for specific education requirements and for professional experience.

APPRENTICESHIP, ACCREDITATION, VALIDATION

Three additional programs have proven to be invaluable to ACF members. ACF offers about 100 three-year culinary and pastry apprenticeship programs throughout the United States. In the past 20 years, more than 18,000 appren-

tices have benefited from working under ACF-approved supervisory chefs in ACF-sponsoring foodservice facilities that range from themed resorts (Walt Disney World, Opryland) to elegant hotels (Atlanta's Ritz-Carlton, Sea Island's The Cloister) to large and small independent restaurants. Upon completion of the program, which is recognized by the U.S. Department of Labor, each graduate earns ACF designation as a certified culinarian (CC).

The ACF Accrediting Commission functions as official accrediting agency for culinary, baking, and pastry educational programs at post-secondary schools throughout the United States. In recent decades, as the culinary profession has earned greater prominence, culinary education has developed at an accelerated rate. Recognizing the need to monitor such programs for quality performance, ACF formed this commission in 1986 to ensure that industry standards are met within educational environments.

ACCESS ACF is a blue-ribbon program of validation for secondary and vocational culinary arts and foodservice programs. As *the* authority on cooking in America, ACF is committed to ensuring that such programs meet industry and professional standards. In addition, *ACCESS ACF* designates any student who graduates from a validated program, passes a written test, and verifies successful completion of an approved sanitation course as a *validated graduate*.

FIGHTING CHILDHOOD HUNGER

American Culinary Federation Chef and Child Foundation (ACF CCF) serves as the voice and the army of ACF in its continuing, unrelenting fight against childhood hunger in the United States. The more than 300 ACF chapters work in their communities to provide nutrition education to pre-school children and youngsters in kindergarten through fifth grade. ACF chefs foster awareness of childhood hunger, poverty, and poor nutrition as they relate to food, and they train and work with agencies that receive and dispense donated foods through food-rescue programs. ACF CCF has been designated a 501(c)3 charity by the U.S. Internal Revenue Service.

WORLDWIDE PARTNERSHIP

Every member of ACF is simultaneously enrolled in the World Association of Cooks Societies (WACS), a global association of millions of chefs and cooks who live and work in 54 nations on five continents. ACF is the representative organization for the United States.

CULINARY TEAMWORK

ACF also manages an official team of exceptional chefs who officially represent the United States in international culinary competitions, the most prestigious of which is Internationale Kochkunst Austellung. Familiarly called the Culinary Olympics, this event was held every four years in Frankfurt, Germany, until 1996, when it moved to Berlin. 1992 Culinary Team USA earned world championship status in five of six competitions. 1996 Culinary Team USA won a total of 58 medals, more than any other competing country.

≈

responsibilities and activities with those of other departments.

A **CEPC**, certified executive pastry chef, functions as head of his or her department and is usually responsible to a CEC of a foodservice operation or to management of a pastry-specialty firm or research company.

A **CCE**, certified culinary educator, is a professional chef who is employed as an educator by the culinary or foodservice-management department of an accredited learning institution. Certification as a CCE requires extensive post-secondary teacher education, in addition to many hours of teaching experience. Each applicant must also possess culinary experience and expertise equal to that of a CSC.

A **CCC**, certified chef de cuisine, is a chef who supervises food production in a foodservice operation, such as one unit of a multi-unit operation or a free-standing operation. He or she is in charge of an operation with final decision-making authority relating to culinary functions. Each applicant must supervise a minimum of three full-time employees engaged in the production of food.

A **CSC**, certified sous chef, supervises a shift, station, or stations in a foodservice operation. He or she must supervise a minimum of two full-time employees who prepare food. Job titles that usually qualify for this designation include sous chef, banquet chef, chef garde manger, first cook, AM or PM sous chef.

A **CWPC**, certified working pastry chef, is responsible for a pastry section or shift within a foodservice operation.

A **CC**, certified culinarian, is positioned in any one station in a foodservice operation and is responsible for preparing and cooking sauces, cold foods, fish, soups and stocks, meats, vegetables, eggs, and other items.

A **CPC**, certified pastry culinarian, is positioned at one station in a foodservice operation and is responsible for preparing and cooking pies, cookies, cakes, breads, rolls, and other baked goods and dessert items.

~Recognition

FIVE ANNUAL AWARDS, AN HONOR SOCIETY, AND A HALL OF FAME

CHEFS OF THE YEAR

ACF takes great pride in listing the 36 recipients of its national Chef of the Year award.

~

1963	Walter Roth, AAC
1964	Jean Michelet, AAC
1965	John Bandera, CEC, AAC
1966	Charles Finance, AAC
1967	Otto Spielbicher*
1968	Ferdinand E, Metz, CMC, AAC
1969	Tom Lockman, AAC
1970	Jan Verdonkschot
1971	Alec Cline, CEC, AAC*
1972	Richard Bosnjak, CEC, AAC
1973	Jack Sullivan*
1974	Rene Roncari*
1975	Eugene Bluenschein*
1976	Bernard Urban, CEC, AAC
1977	Jack F. Braun, CEC, AAC
1978	Ray Marshall, AAC*
1979	Baron H. Galand, CEC, AAC*
1980	Henry Michael*
1981	Lawrence A. Conti, CEC, AAC*
1982	Jeff Larson, CEC, AAC
1983	Hermann Rusch, AAC*
1984	U. Max Behr, CEC, AAC
1985	Richard Schneider, CMC, AAC
1986	Jon Greenwalt, CEC, AAC
1987	Leon Oppenheimer*
1988	Bert P. Cutino, CEC, AAC
1989	Michel Bouit, CEC, AAC
1990	John Folse, CEC, AAC
1991	Roland E. Schaeffer, CEC, AAC
1992	Reimund D. Pitz, CEC, CCE, AAC
1993	Hartmut Handke, CMC, AAC
1994	Fritz Sonnenschmidt, CMC, AAC
1995	George O'Palenick, CEC, CCE, AAC
1996	Carl Huckaby, CEC, CCE, AAC
1997	Michael Ty, CEC, AAC
1998	L. Timothy Ryan, CMC, AAC

* deceased

ACF CHEF OF THE YEAR

The highest honor that can be earned by an ACF member is Chef of the Year. This annual award was introduced in 1963 to honor a culinarian who has distinguished himself or herself in the foodservice profession and who has worked vigorously to promote and advance the profession.

To be considered for the award, a chef or culinary educator must have been certified by ACF, have served as an officer of his or her chapter, have participated extensively in charitable projects, have demonstrated exceptional dedication to the profession, and have been named chef of the year in his or her region. The award is sponsored by Tyson Foods, Inc.

(ABOVE) AT THE 1997 ACF NATIONAL CONVENTION, ALL PAST NATIONAL CHEF OF THE YEAR RECIPIENTS WERE RECOGNIZED AND 17 WHO WERE IN ATTENDANCE WERE PRESENTED WITH A SPECIALLY COMMISSIONED GOLD RING. (LEFT) 1998 CHEF OF THE YEAR L. TIMOTHY RYAN, CMC, AAC, ACCEPTED THE AWARD FROM ACF NATIONAL PRESIDENT NOEL CULLEN, ED.D., CMC, AAC, AND AWARDS CHAIR CHARLES HASTREITER, CEC, AAC.

CHEF PROFESSIONALISM AWARD

Each year, too, ACF presents a Chef Professionalism Award to its member who best represents the highest standards of professionalism in the foodservice industry. Each of the four annual candidates has earned the Chef Professionalsm Award for his or her region. Members of the selection committee, composed of past regional finalists, base their decision on five major areas of accomplishment: certification, continuing education and training, participation in culinary competitions, contributions to the development of aspiring culinarians, and involvement in community service. The award is sponsored by Minor's, a division of Nestlé FoodServices.

JUNIOR MEMBER OF THE YEAR

ACF established its Junior Member of the Year Award in 1987, at the recommendation of the late Baron H. Galand, CEC, AAC. Its purpose is to recognize stellar accomplishments by young culinarians. Each candidate must be nominated by his or her chapter president and must have been a junior member of ACF for one to four years. And, to be considered, each must prepare and submit a file documenting education, training, employment, and participation (as a volunteer) in charitable and community events.

EDUCATOR OF THE YEAR

In 1995, ACF created this citation to honor active educators whose culinary knowledge, skills, expertise, and exemplary dedication have enhanced the image of professional chefs and who, by example, have provided leadership, guidance, and direction to students who aspire to culinary careers. Recipients demonstrate the ability to provide strong foundations that will help students define and develop career goals based on their own skills and abilities.

HERMANN RUSCH MEMORIAL AWARD

Since 1993, at the discretion of ACF's national president, the federation has honored five members who have contributed immeasurably to the development, growth, activities, and ideals of their chapters. Each recipient's involvement in his chapter's culinary and charitable events has contributed directly to the advancement of the culinary profession.

CHEF PROFESSIONALISM AWARDS

ACF proudly salutes the distinguished recipients of the national Chef Professionalism Award:

1990	Roland Henin, CMC, CCE, AAC
1991	Roland E. Schaeffer, CEC, AAC
1992	Hartmut Handke, CMC, AAC
1993	Walter Rhea, CMPC, CEC, CCE, AAC
1994	Johnny Rivers, CEC, AAC
1995	Joseph Amendola, CEPC, CCE, AAC
1996	Noble Masi, CEPC, AAC
1997	Clayton Sherrod, CEC, AAC
1998	Deborah J. Trudeau, CCE

JUNIOR MEMBERS OF THE YEAR

ACF celebrates the following national Junior Members of the Year:

1987	Denise Fullmer Murray
1988	Steven John Buffone
1989	Thomas Madara
1990	Robert Cawley
1991	Patricia Thibodeau
1992	John Munson
1993	Annette Lehner
1994	Catherine Givens Duehlmier
1995	Adrienne Novak
1996	Jennifer L. Salmon
1997	Lon Symensma
1998	Thomas Joseph Gribben, Jr.

EDUCATORS OF THE YEAR

ACF honors:

1995	Noel Cullen, Ed.D., CMC, AAC
1998	Ferdinand E. Metz, CMC, AAC

HERMANN RUSCH MEMORIAL AWARDS

ACF pays tribute to:

1993	Hermann G. Rusch, AAC
1994	Willy Rossel, AAC
1996	George Hirsch, CEC, CCE, AAC
1997	Bert P. Cutino, CEC, AAC
1998	Lawrence A. Conti, CEC, AAC

THE AMERICAN ACADEMY OF CHEFS

The AAC is honored to cite recipients of its chairman's medal:

~

1976	Christian Inden, AAC
1977	Otto Spielbichler, AAC*
1978	Anthony C. Bartolatta, AAC*
1979	Rene Roncari, AAC
1980	Paul Laesecke, AAC*
1981	Baron H. Galand, CEC, AAC*
1982	Richard Rosnjak, CEC, AAC
1983	Ferdinand E. Metz, CMC, AAC
1984	Richard Schneider, CMC, AAC
1985	Jon Greenwalt, CEC, AAC
1986	Alec O. Kline, CEC, AAC
1987	Hermann Rusch, AAC*
1988	Willy Rossel, AAC
1989	Lawrence A. Conti, CEC, AAC*
1990	Jack F. Braun, CEC, AAC
1991	Casey Sinkeldam, CMPC, CEC, AAC
1992	U. Max Behr, CEC, AAC
1993	Harry H. Hoffstadt, CEC, AAC
1994	William Moore, CEC, AAC
1995	L. Edwin Brown
1996	John Folse, CEC, AAC
1997	Michael Ty, CEC, AAC
1998	Roland E. Schaeffer, CEC, AAC

* deceased

THE AMERICAN ACADEMY OF CHEFS

If for no other reason, the 1955 ACF national convention in Pittsburgh will be remembered because delegates voted to establish The American Academy of Chefs, the American Culinary Federation's official honor society. Its purpose is to recognize ACF chefs and culinary educators who have excelled in their professions.

To earn the right to list AAC after his or her name, an ACF member must have fulfilled all requirements for election to membership in the academy, including completion of 10 of twenty mandatory goals. All candidates must be also present for induction during a national convention.

Members of the AAC have practiced the highest standards and have demonstrated the highest qualities of professionalism within ACF, in their communities, and in the foodservice industry. They also promote education to all who follow them in the profession and pass on the skills and expertise they have developed. And, they project positive images at the local, regional, and national culinary and charitable events that they enthusiastically support, attend, and sponsor.

Since 1988, the AAC has also elected 37 of its members to its Hall of Fame. In the words of the late Hermann Rusch, AAC, the purpose of the AAC Hall of Fame is "to honor those men and women who, because of their outstanding attributes, have won the respect and love of their professional guild… they are so honored by their peers as a positive reflection to all those in this profession who seek achievement."

Eight other foodservice professionals have been inducted as honorary members of the AAC Hall of Fame. In addition, 23 foodservice professionals have been named honorary members of AAC. Not all honorary members of the Hall of Fame and the AAC are ACF members, nor does their honorary status, in and of itself, entitle any to list AAC after his or her name.

In addition, each year since 1978, an AAC chairman's medal has been presented in recognition of exemplary dedication and contributions to the culinary profession, maintenance of the highest standards and ideals of the AAC, and relentless work to assure excellence among future culinarians.

NEW MEMBERS OF THE AMERICAN ACADEMY OF CHEFS ARE INDUCTED INTO THE HONOR SOCIETY AT A CEREMONY HELD DURING THE ACF NATIONAL CONVENTION.

THE AUTHORITY ON *Cooking* IN AMERICA

LEARNING WHILE COOKING

COMPETITIONS AS EDUCATIONAL EXPERIENCES

Ask a dozen gold-medal winners of professional culinary competitions what factors play significant roles in earning points in ACF cookoffs and you will hear 12 different opinions. Scoring criteria, however, reveal priorities.

Officially, ACF sanctions/sponsors/supports 35 types of professional culinary competitions—11 of which are cold-food exhibits in which entries are not tasted—plus five kinds of ice-carving meets. For 24 of the formats—all hot-food events—judges rank flavor as the single most important standard.

Still, a high score for taste alone cannot turn an entry into a winner. Superior flavor must be wedded to excellent texture and correct doneness—then combined with creativity, menu/ingredient compatibility, appropriate portioning, balanced nutrition, proper service, and appealing presentation.

In addition, in hot-food cookoffs, kitchen performance—cooking skills, techniques, and knowledge of fundamentals—is evaluated. Judges also consider *mise en place* or organization, sanitation procedures and cleanliness, apprentice coordination and task delegation, effective utilization of all ingredients, and timing of service and follow-up.

No chef decides on a whim to enter a culinary competition. Weeks of research, planning, preparation, and practice are required, for cookoffs are grueling, to say the least. Competitors tend to be ambitious, intensely motivated, creative, committed, determined, and focused on every detail of a competitive challenge. And, certainly, their culinary skills are finely honed.

Winners agree that professional cookoffs are one-of-a-kind educational opportunities. Chefs enter to learn, they say, and to stretch their creativity and demonstrate technical expertise. Much of the learning, they add, occurs during before-cookoff research and after-cookoff critiques by judges.

According to Roland E. Schaeffer, CEC, AAC—who may have evaluated more entries than any other ACF-certified judge—culinary competitions afford unique opportunities for chefs and students to develop skills, share knowledge and innovations, launch trends, and teach professionals as well as consumers. "Competitions," he added, "are educational showcases for culinary artistry."

In addition to sponsors' prizes, ACF presents medals and diplomas to high-scoring competitors. All medals are numbered, and names of recipients are recorded in a permanent registry. And, points for each medal earned may be applied toward a competitor's ACF certification education requirements.

~

ACF COMPETITION AWARDS

~

The following awards can be earned at national, regional, chapter, and local competitions:

ACF gold medal for 36 to 40 points

ACF silver medal for 32 to 35.99 points

ACF bronze medal for 28 to 31.99 points

ACF culinary diploma for 24 to 27.99 points

TASTE IS PARAMOUNT; BUT CULINARY COMPETITORS ARE ALSO JUDGED ON COOKING TECHNIQUES, ORGANIZATION, SANITATION PROCEDURES, AND TASK DELEGATION.

1998 ENTRY IN THE FIFTH ANNUAL ACF NATIONAL SOUP & SAUCE CHAMPIONSHIP SPONSORED BY CUSTOM FOOD PRODUCTS: VEAL CHOPS WITH WILD MUSHROOM-SWEET POTATO HASH BY ERIC OLSON, CEC.

Directory of Knowledgeable Culinary Professionals

Each of the following ACF national officers and chairs can be reached through the national office of the American Culinary Federation, 10 San Bartola Drive, St. Augustine, FL 32086.
Telephone (800) 624-9458 or (904) 824-4468
Fax (904) 825-4758, e-mail acf@acfchefs.net

ELECTED OFFICERS

President ....Noel Cullen, Ed.D., CMC, AAC
Chairman of the Board...Reimund D. Pitz, CEC, CCE, AAC
Secretary ....John Kinsella, CMC, CCE, AAC
Treasurer ....George J. Pastor, Ed.D., CEC, CCE, AAC
American Academy of Chefs Chairman ....Burt P. Cutino, CEC, AAC
American Academy of Chefs Secretary-Treasurer.............Fritz Sonnenschmidt, CMC, AAC
Vice President/Central Region ....Michel D. Bouit, CEC, AAC
Vice President/Northeast Region ....Edward G. Leonard, CMC, AAC
Vice President/Southeast Region...................................Klaus D. Friedenreich, CMC, AAC
Vice President/Western Region ....Bob Chester, CEC, CCE, AAC

APPOINTED CHAIRS

Accreditation..Joel Tanner, CEC, AAC
Apprenticeship..Thomas J. Macrina, CEC, AAC
Bylaws and Resolutions ....John M. Lundbom, CEC
Certification...Walter N. Bronowitz, CCC, CCE, AAC
Culinary Competitions...Steven Jilleba, CMC, CCE, AAC
Education ....Paul Sorgule, CCE
Ethics...Joseph Amabile, CCC
Government Affairs ....Damian Martineau, CEC, AAC
History ....Willy Rossel, AAC
Internal Audit...George O'Palenick, CEC, CCE, AAC
Junior Membership..Elizabeth A. Baase, CWC
Membership/Chapter Relations ....Harry Brockwell, CEC, AAC
National Awards..Charles A. Hastreiter, CEC, AAC
Nominations and Elections ....Steven Ward
Parliamentarian ....Reed S. Miller, Jr.
Public Relations ....Richard P. Nickless, CEC
Seal of Approval..James Taylor, CEC, AAC
Senior Chefs...Joseph Amendola, CEPC, CCE, AAC
Sergeant-at-Arms...Bruce Riddell, CEC, AAC

ACCESS ACF ....James Griffin, CEC, CCE
ACF Planning...Gerard Murphy
ACF Benefits ....Bobby Lee Elliott, CEC, AAC
ACF Technology ....George Cook, Jr.
President's Advisory Council for National Convention.....Michael Ty, CEC, AAC

 *Menu of Culinary Terms*

amaretto. Almond-flavored liqueur, a sweet alcoholic beverage made from an infusion of flavoring ingredients and a spirit such as brandy, rum, or whiskey.

Arborio rice. Grown in Italy, this rice has kernels that are shorter and fatter than any other short-grain rice. Its high-starch content produces the creamy texture of risotto.

arrowroot. A thickening agent for puddings, sauces, and other cooked foods. Its thickening power is about twice that of flour, and it has no flavor and becomes clear when cooked.

baguette. French bread baked in a very long, thin cylindrical loaf, usually crisp and brown outside, soft and chewy inside.

balsamic vinegar. Made from white Trebbiano grape juice, this beautifully flavored vinegar is aged in wooden barrels, which process imparts its dark color.

Barolo. Italian red wine with exceptional bouquet and robust body, made from Nebbiolo grapes grown in the Piedmont region.

biscotti (singular: biscotto). Very crunchy twice-baked Italian biscuits (or cookies) that are first baked in a loaf or cake, which is sliced, and then the slices are baked again. Flavorings are almost limitless. Biscotti are often dipped into dessert wine or coffee.

black trumpet mushroom. Flesh is thin, brittle, buttery-flavored, aromatic, and ranges from greyish brown to almost black. Shaped like a trumpet, this mushrooms grows from 2" to 5" high.

blanch. To plunge vegetables or fruits into boiling water briefly, drain, and plunge into cold water to stop the cooking process. Purposes of blanching are to firm the flesh, loosen skins (especially of tomatoes and peaches), and heighten and set color

and flavor before freezing.

borscht. Soup made from fresh beets, indigenous to Poland and Russia. Other vegetables are usually included and, in some versions, meat and meat stock. Most recipes can be served hot or cold, and most are garnished with sour cream.

brazier or rondeau. A pan—usually round with two handles and a tight-fitting lid—designed for braising.

brunoise. Finely diced vegetables that have been slowly cooked in butter and will be used to flavor a soup or sauce.

capellini. Very fine pasta, but not as fine as capelli d'angelo (angel hair).

cardamom. Member of ginger family having long, light green or brown pods, each containing a seed with strong, lemony flavor, hints of camphor, and pleasantly pungent aroma.

caul. A thin, fatty membrane that lines the abdominal cavity. It resembles a lacy net and is used to wrap and hold together pâtès, crépinettes, and forcemeats. During cooking, the fatty membrane melts.

caviar. Sieved, lightly salted fish roe. Three main types: beluga (the most expensive), pale silver to black, considered the best, from the beluga sturgeon that live in the Caspian Sea; osetra, grey to brownish grey; and sevruga, grey. Other caviars include sterlet (golden and rare), lumpfish, whitefish, and salmon or red.

celeriac. The root of a variety of celery, also called celery root and celery knob, that is cultivated for its root. Size ranges from that of an apple to a small cantaloupe. Taste resembles a combination of celery and parsley.

chanterelle. Trumpet-shaped wild mushroom with ruffled-edge cap; yellow-orange color; smooth, slightly chewy texture; distinctive nutty, fruity

flavor; and clean, earthy aroma.

chiffonade. Thin strips or shreds of leafy vegetables either sautéed lightly or added raw as a garnish to soups.

Chinese cabbage. An oblong head of crinkly, thickly veined leaves whose color ranges from celadon to cream. Unlike more common round-headed cabbage, this variety has thin leaves that are crisp and delicately mild. Also called Napa cabbage, bakusai, celery cabbage, wong bok, and Peking cabbage.

chipolata sausage. Small, spicy 2" to 3" long sausage made from pork, thyme, chives, coriander, cloves, and sometimes hot red-pepper flakes.

cilantro. Bright green leaves and stems of coriander plant. Also called Chinese parsley and coriander leaf.

colcannon. From Ireland, mashed potatoes mixed with cooked kale or cabbage, scallions, butter, milk, and sometimes parsley.

concassé. Coarsely chopped vegetable or vegetables, especially tomatoes.

confit. A technique that originated in southwestern France for preserving poultry or meat that has been cooked in its own fat and stored in a pot covered with its fat.

coulis. Thick purée or sauce; e.g., tomato coulis.

court-bouillon. An aromatic vegetable broth that usually includes an acidic ingredient, such as wine or vinegar; most commonly used for poaching fish.

couscous. Granular semolina (durum wheat that is more coarsely ground than most wheat flours) that is a staple in North Africa where, after cooking, it is served with milk as porridge, with dressing as salad, or sweetened and mixed with fruits as dessert.

crème fraîche. Matured, thickened cream with a slightly tangy, nutty flavor and rich, velvety texture.

cremino (plural: cremini). Dark brown, somewhat firmer variety of cultivated white mushroom with full flavor. Also called common brown and Roman mushroom.

crudités. Crisp raw vegetables served as appetizers with dipping sauces.

curaçao. Orange-flavored liqueur made from dried peel of bitter oranges grown in Curaçao, an island in the Caribbean Sea.

curly endive. Often mistakenly called chicory, curly endive grows in loose heads of lacy, green-rimmed outer leaves that curl at their ends. Off-white center leaves form a compact heart. Texture is slightly prickly; flavor is slightly bitter.

daikon. A large (6" to 15" long and 2" to 3" in diameter) Asian radish with sweet, fresh flavor and crisp, juicy, white flesh. Its skin can be either cream-colored or black.

dariole. A small, deep mold for pastries, flans, babas, vegetable custards, and rice pudding, or an item prepared in such a mold.

deglaze. To heat a small amount of liquid (usually stock or wine) in a pan in which food (usually meat or poultry) has been sautéed or browned and from which the food and any excess fat have been removed. While heating, the pan is stirred and scraped to loosen browned bits of food. The resulting liquid is used as a base for sauce to accompany the the sautéed or browned food.

demi-glace. Made from basic espagnole (brown) sauce, beef stock, and Madeira or sherry, all cooked until reduced by half to a thick glaze that coats a spoon. Used as base for many sauces because of its intense flavor.

emulsion. Mixture of two liquids that do not combine easily, such as oil and water or oil and vinegar. The two liquids must be whisked together vigorously to create the desired thick, satiny texture. This requires adding oil gradually, almost drop by drop.

escarole. An endive with broad, slightly curved, pale-green leaves. Escarole has a milder, less bitter flavor than either Belgian or curly endive. Also called Batavian endive.

egg wash. A mixture of beaten eggs, yolks, or whites and milk or water, for coating doughs before baking in order to add sheen.

forcemeat. Finely ground (usually several times to achieve smooth texture) meat, poultry, seafood, vegetables, or fruit (raw or cooked) mixed with bread crumbs and seasonings. Forcemeat is used as stuffing or to make quenelles (small oval dumplings).

french. To cut vegetables or meats lengthwise into very thin strips. Or, to cut meat away from the end of a rib or chop to expose part of the bone.

gateau. The French word for cake, whether plain or fancy. Plural form is gateaux.

Gorgonzola. Named for a town near Milan where it was made originally, this cow's-milk cheese is ivory-colored and lightly streaked with bluish-green. Gorgonzola is creamy and rich; it has a savory, pungent flavor.

grappa. A high-alcohol Italian spirit distilled from residue left in wine presses after juice is removed. Muscato grappa is created from Muscat grapes.

gravlax. Raw salmon cured—in Sweden where it originated—in a mixture of salt, sugar, and dill. It is sliced very thin for serving, traditionally, on dark bread as an appetizer or an open-faced sandwich.

Guinness. Dark, heavy-bodied stout (a type of beer) originating in Dublin, Ireland, in 1759. Stout is made with roasted malt (barley) and more hops (cones of a vine) than other beers; the process produces robust beer with deep color and bittersweet flavor.

haricots verts. Young, very slender green beans with dull green, tender pods and very small seeds. Also called French green beans and French beans.

Italian parsley. A variety of parsley with flat, darker green leaves and a stronger flavor than standard curly parsley. Also called flat-leaf parsley.

Irish whiskey. Triple-distilled whiskey made in Ireland from the same fermented grains used in Scotland to produce Scotch whisky (no "e" in Scotland). The Irish, however, do not smoke-cure the grains, which results in smooth, full-bodied whiskey with a clean, malty flavor.

julienne. A term for foods that have been cut into thin matchlike strips and for the knife technique required to create the strips.

kirsch. Also called kirschwasser (meaning, in German, cherry water), this clear brandy is distilled from cherry juice and pits.

kale. Member of the cabbage family with curly leaves formed into a loose bunch. Colors range from pale to dark green tinged with lavender, blue, or purple, to white shaded with pink, purple, or green. Green varieties are best for cooking, others for garnishing.

lardons. Narrow strips of fat used to bard lean meats, or pork or bacon that has been diced, blanched, and fried. Sometimes spelled lardoons.

lemon thyme. A subvariety of wild thyme that grows as a ground cover and has a more pronounced lemon aroma than garden thyme.

mandoline. A small hand-operated tool with several adjustable blades with which to slice foods in various thicknesses, often used for julienne and French-fry cutting.

mascarpone cheese. Buttery, rich double- to triple-cream cheese made from cow's milk and originating in Lombardy, Italy. Ivory-colored, soft, and delicate, the cheese has a texture ranging from that of clotted cream to room-temperature butter.

mesclun. Salad mix of young, small

greens—arugula, dandelion, frisée, mizuma, oak leaf, mâche, radicchio, sorrel, et al.

millet. A cereal grass that is a staple of most of the world's population, except in the United States where it is cultivated mostly for fodder and bird seed. The many varieties of millet are rich in protein and have bland flavors that benefit from seasonings. Millet is cooked like rice and used to prepare hot cereal, pilaf, and other dishes. When ground, it is also used as flour for puddings, breads, and cakes.

mirepoix. Mixture of diced carrots, onions, celery, and herbs (and sometimes ham or bacon) sautéed in butter, to be used to season sauces, soups, and stews, or to serve as a bed on which to braise meat or fish.

mise en place. French for putting in place. The term is used to describe the assembling and preparing of all necessary ingredients and equipment for creating a dish, course, or meal.

morel. An edible wild mushroom of the same fungus species as a truffle. The morel's spongy, honeycombed, cone-shaped cap ranges from 2 to 4 inches high. Its flavor is smoky, earthy, and slightly nutty. In general the darker the color (from tan to brown) the stronger the flavor.

mortar. Small bowl-shaped container usually used with a pestle (a rounded, batlike instrument) to pulverize spices, herbs, and other foods. The two can be made from marble, hardwood, porcelain, or stoneware.

muesli. Breakfast cereal developed as a health food in Switzerland. Can include raw or toasted cereals (oats, wheat, millet, barley, et al.), dried fruits, nuts, bran, wheat germ, sugar, and dried-milk solids. Now often labeled granola.

noisette. Small, tender, round slice of meat from rib or loin of lamb, veal, or beef.

oyster mushroom. A fan-shaped mushroom, whose cap color varies from pale grey to dark brownish-grey, that grows wild and is cultivated. Also called oyster cap, tree mushroom, tree oyster mushroom, summer oyster mushroom, pleurotte, and shimeji.

pancetta. Unsmoked Italian bacon cured with salt and spices.

Pernod. French licorice-flavored pastis (aperitif), similar to absinthe but made without oil of wormwood.

phyllo. Tissue-thin layers of pastry dough traditionally used in Greek and Near Eastern sweet and savory dishes—e.g., baklava, spanakopita. Similar to strudel.

pine nut. High-fat nut from several varieties of pine trees. Also called pignoli (Italian), pignon (French), Indian nut, and pignolia. Used in a variety of savory and sweet dishes. Essential to classic Italian pesto.

Pinot Noir. The red grape from which spicy, rich, complex red Burgundies from France and Pinot Noirs from California, Oregon, and Washington are produced. It is also an ingredient in French champagnes and U.S. sparkling wines. Pinot Noirs pair well with most foods.

pissaladière. A tart with flaky crust topped with onions, anchovies, ripe olives, tomatoes, and/or other ingredients. A specialty of Nice in southern France.

poivrade. Designation for any sauce in which peppercorns provide the dominant flavor.

porcino (plural: porcini). A pale brown wild mushroom that can weigh from 1 ounce to 1 pound. Also called a cèpe.

portobello mushroom. An extremely large, dark brown mushroom that is actually a fully mature cremino.

prawn. 1. Species of crustacean in lobster family—e.g., Dublin Bay prawn, Danish lobster, Italian scampi, French langoustine, Spanish langostino, Caribbean lobsterette, Florida lobsterette—with a body shaped like a tiny Maine lobster. 2. Freshwater counterpart of saltwater shrimp that looks like a cross between a shrimp and a lobster. 3. Jumbo shrimp—15 or fewer to a pound.

puff pastry or *pâté feuilletée*. Rich, delicate, flaky, pastry created by dotting layers of dough with cold fat (usually butter), rolling each layer, folding it in thirds, letting it rest, and repeating the techniques six to eight times. During baking, the pastry rises and separates into hundreds of layers. Puff pastry is used to make *allumettes*, *croissants*, Napoleons, *palmiers*, tart shells, *vol-au-vents*, *fleurons*, and as wrappings for meats, seafoods, cheeses, and fruits.

radicchio. Red-leafed Italian chicory usually used as salad green. Two varieties most common in the United States: radicchio di Verona with small, loose heads of white-ribbed burgundy-colored leaves; and radicchio di Treviso with lighter, more tapered heads of white-ribbed leaves that range from pink to dark red.

ramekin. Small ceramic soufflé dish with 4-ounce capacity, or a small baked pastry with a creamy cheese filling.

ravier. Flat, boat-shaped china plate, used in France for serving hors d'oeuvre.

render or try out. To melt animal fat away from its meat (such as bacon) over low heat. Melted fat separates from connective tissue (meat), which becomes brown and crisp and is usually referred to as cracklings.

rice wine. Sweet, gold-colored, low-alcohol-content wine made from fermented steamed glutinous rice. Japanese rice wines: sake and mirin. Chinese rice wines: Chia Fan, Hsiang Hsueh, Shan Niang, and Yen Hung.

risotto. A rice specialty from Italy, prepared by gradually stirring hot stock into Arborio rice and onions that have been sautéed in butter or olive oil and by stirring almost constantly and cooking until all liquid has been absorbed. The result is delicately creamy, yet the grains of rice remain firm and separated from each other. Risottos can be flavored with shellfish, sausage, chicken, vegetables, cheese, wine, herbs, et al. The most famous, risotto Milanese, is seasoned with saffron.

roux. Mixture of flour and fat that is slowly cooked over low heat and used to thicken sauces, gravies, and soups. Three classic roux: white, blond, brown. Color and flavor of sauce is determined by length of time the roux is cooked.

royale. Custard cooked in a dariole, usually cut into shapes and used to garnish clear soup.

sambuca. Anise-flavored, slightly sweet Italian liqueur, usually served with two or three dark-roasted coffee beans floating on top.

savoy cabbage. Mellow-flavored, loose-headed, crinkly leafed cabbage.

sec. French for dry.

shiitake. Mushroom originating in Japan and Korea, now cultivated in the United States as well. Dark brown cap can be 8" to 10" across, although average is 3" to 6" in diameter. Tough stems are usually used to add flavor to stocks and sauces, then discarded. Caps have full-bodied, woody flavor. Shiitakes are available fresh and dried.

slurry. Thin paste of water and cornstarch or flour that is whisked into hot liquids (soup, sauce, stew, et al.) as thickener. The mixture is then cooked and whisked until it comes to a boil and the thickening loses its raw taste.

sorrel. A family of hardy herbs with some acidity and sourness. Leaves are shaped like spinach, can be from 2 to 12" long. Color varies from pale to dark green. Peak season is spring.

stir-fry. To fry small pieces of food quickly in a wok or skillet while constantly stirring. This technique requires little fat and produces crisply tender food.

sultana. Small, pale golden-green grape originating in Turkey, cultivated today primarily for raisins.

sweat. To cook vegetables in a small amount of fat over low heat—to soften without browning and to cook in their own juices.

tapenade. A thick paste, from the Provence region of France, made from capers, anchovies, ripe olives, olive oil, lemon juice, seasonings, and often tuna. Tapenade is used as a condiment or spread or served with crudités, fish, meat, poultry, and other dishes.

tat-soi. An Asian cabbage with unusually mild flavor. The leaves resemble those of Brussels sprouts. When very young, tat-soi is used in salads.

temper. To bring an ingredient to proper temperature or texture by mixing, stirring, heating, or cooling; e.g., eggs tempered by whisking in a little hot liquid to prevent curdling.

terrine. 1. Ground seasoned meats baked in a mold and served cold. 2. Ground seasoned meat, seafood, poultry, and/or vegetable forcemeat baked in a mold and served hot or cold (e.g., pâté). 3. The mold (earthenware, metal, or glass) in which such mixtures are baked—often a rectangular pan with a flared edge.

tofu. Also called soybean curd and bean curd, tofu is made from curdled soy milk that has been extracted from ground cooked soybeans, is high in iron content, and looks somewhat like firm, smooth, white custard. Popular in the Orient, especially in Japan, tofu tastes bland but slightly nutty and takes on the flavor of the food with which it is cooked.

tortellini. Small stuffed pasta, shaped into rings or hats. Larger versions are called tortelloni.

tourné. A vegetable, especially a potato or mushroom, that has been turned or shaped with a knife.

turmeric. Dried powdery spice with strong, spicy flavor and yellow color used in Indian and Middle Eastern cuisines and as a yellow coloring agent. Also called Indian saffron.

velouté. One of the five "mother" sauces. A white sauce based on stock—usually chicken, veal, or seafood—rather than milk and thickened with a white roux. Velouté can be enriched by the addition of egg yolk(s) and/or cream and can serve as the foundation for other sauces.

water bath or bain marie. A cooking technique consisting of placing a pan, bowl, soufflé dish, etc., of food in a large, shallow pan of warm water, which surrounds the container of food with gentle heat. Food is usually cooked by this method in an oven, or it can be cooked on top of a stove. This technique cooks delicate dishes—custards, sauces, savory mousses—without breaking them down or curdling them; it is also used to keep cooked foods warm.

whisk. Kitchen utensil in various sizes and shapes (e.g., balloon, flat, sauce, and trimmed whisks) consisting of wire loops joined at a handle. Loops usually form a round or teardrop shape. Also known as a whip, the tool is used to incorporate air into foods and to create an emulsion.

≈

Bibliography for glossary:
1. The author/editor's own knowledge.
2. Herbst, Sharon Tyler. The New Food Lover's Companion. *2nd edition. Hauppauge, NY, : Barron's Educational Series, 1995.*
3. Labensky, Steven, and Gaye G. Ingram and Sarah R. Labensky. Webster's New World Dictionary of Culinary Arts. *Upper Saddle River, NJ: Prentice Hall, 1997.*
4. Riely, Elizabeth. The Chef's Companion. *New York: Van Nostrand Reinhold, 1986.*

≈ 70 Years of ≈
PIONEERING AND PROFESSIONALISM

OTHER PHOTOGRAPHY CREDITS

Acknowledgement is made for all photographs not taken specifically for the purpose of this work: ACF Archives, page 7 (top); Culinary Archives & Museum (CA&M), page 7 (middle and bottom); CA&M, page 8 (top right); ACF Archives, page 9 (bottom); CA&M, page 9 (top right); CA&M, page 10 (bottom); CA&M, page 11 (top); ACF Archives, page 12 (all except bottom left); CA&M, page 12 (bottom left); CA&M, page 13 (top); ACF Archives, page 14 (top and bottom); ACF Archives, page 15 (bottom); ACF Archives, page 17 (bottom right); ACF Archives, page 70 (bottom left and right); Walter Coker, page 72 (top left); ACF Archives, page 72 (bottom right); ACF Archives, page 73 (top right); Custom Food Products, page 73 (bottom right).